No Longer Orphans

Journey into the Father's Heart

James S. Macchi

Printed in the United States of America
ISBN: 978-0-9860996-0-1

James Macchi
jamesmacchi271@gmail.com
Rejoice Ministries International
www.rejoiceministriesinternational.com

ENDORSEMENTS

"James Macchi is a man who is aflame with and exudes God's multi-faceted love in special ways. He is experienced, engaging, discerning, hopeful, generous, clear and focused on glorifying our heavenly Father in every way he can. He carries a living and powerful testimony of being set free from this "orphan spirit" that he exposes so well in this book. James is a marvelous comrade in the kingdom of God who passionately, consistently and daily pursues, with a disarming and childlike wonder, the unfolding revelation of God's nature for his own spiritual growth. And... he faithfully pursues the people that Christ has put in his life to bless and influence without a thought for what he might get back from them. He is both whole and holy without any of the trappings of self-generated religiosity. I love these things about my friend, James Macchi. May God use his book to liberate you from any vestiges of fear, insecurity or despair that would keep you from "finding home" in our Father's heart and receiving the even richer inheritance in Christ that is available to us through the Holy Spirit here and now."

Michael Sullivant, pastor, teacher, speaker
Author, *Prophetic Etiquette, Your Kingdom Come,*
The Romance of Romans

'Wow! Powerful! Anointed! Life-giving! How else can I possibly describe what went off inside of me as I read *No Longer Orphans: Journey into the Father's Heart*. Since the early days of our friendship, over ten years ago, it was obvious to me that the author, James Macchi, was carrying a life message that needed to be shared with the body of Christ. My beloved friend, Jim, bleeds the reality of the rich truths that are proclaimed throughout the pages of this book. So many Christians tragically are being held in captivity to Satan's lies as a result of life's difficult and painful experiences. Every follower of Christ will be strengthened by the rich truths and powerful testimonies within the pages of *No Longer Orphans: Journey into the Father's Heart*."

Richard Dungan
Founder
Rejoice Ministries International

ACKNOWLEDGMENTS

With special thanks:

To Dale Jimmo for help with final formatting to prepare for printing and publishing.

To Richard Dungan, I greatly appreciate our friendship. You are a wonderful encourager and I am blessed to be a part of the ministry of Rejoice Ministries, Intl.

To my wife, Donna, who did the amazing artwork for the front and back cover of this book that so captures the heart of the Father, the Shepherd.

To Philip Ortiz for his gifted photograph and artistry preparing the front and back cover for publishing.

To my incredible ghostwriter/editor, Kathy Borsa, for the many hours that she spent bringing this book together, structuring it, and preparing it for publication, and to our editor, Leslie Valencourt, for her expertise in editing as well as her many encouraging words. Thank you both for sharing the gifts God has given you to help bring this book to completion and for desiring to catch the fire of this work and spread it to others so that they, too, can know that they are no longer orphans but are beloved sons and daughters of the Father.

DEDICATION

I dedicate this book:

To my beautiful and amazing wife and best friend, Donna Marie. You have been my greatest joy and encourager as I have charted these unknown waters as a writer. You have listened to my thoughts and helped bring clarity at times when it all seemed to be a fog. Not only are you an incredible wife but a wonderful Noni (grandmother) to our seven grandchildren. Thank you for your prayers—I could not have done it without your loving support. You are the light and song in my life bringing so much joy to my heart.

To my sons, Adam and Seth—a father could never have asked for better sons. You have grown into men in whom the Father is well pleased. Taking the torch of fatherhood, you are both incredible dads creating a safe environment in which each of your children can develop into the men and women God has called them to be. I am so proud of you both. You are also both amazing husbands to our beautiful daughters in love, Leya and Sarah, who are both incredible moms and wives. My life has been enriched by each and every one of my family members, and I am so thankful for the wonderful gift of your lives that the Father has given to me.

Finally my heart is overwhelmed with gratitude to my heavenly Father who has loved me all the days of my life—who has been with me in the season of "great suffering" and in the joys of new life. You have blessed me in ways that I would never have expected. As your beloved son, I want to thank you with every part of my being. This book is for Your glory and for the purpose of bringing others into a greater understanding of who You truly are and who they truly are in You. Thank You for embracing me with Your love and giving me the opportunity and passion to share Your truth with others.

TABLE OF CONTENTS

INTRODUCTION

…"Let the beloved of the Lord rest secure in Him, for He shields him all day long, and the one the Lord loves rests between His shoulders." (Deut. 33:12 NIV)

Join me on the journey of a lifetime as we seek together to comprehend what is the Father's heart concerning His relationship with you.

In this the love of God was manifested toward us, that God has sent His only begotten Son into the world, that we might live through Him. (1 John 4:9) As we explore the unfathomable nature and character of our Heavenly Father, our discoveries will help us to develop a vibrant relationship with Him. This journey will not stop when you get to the end of the book but will continue through the eternal ages as you increasingly realize the depths of His love and are filled with His fullness.

That Christ may dwell in your hearts through faith; that you, being rooted and grounded in love, may be able to comprehend with all the saints what is the width and length and depth and height—to know the love of Christ which passes knowledge; that you may be filled with all the fullness of God. (Eph. 3:17-19)

The following pages include testimonies shared by individuals who have encountered the heart of the Father and now have a vibrant and growing relationship with Him. Every life encounter, every story, and every parable contains a revelation of the nature and character of the

Father. The intended purpose for each person was to set them free—free to be the unique individual God created them to be.

Moved by the Holy Spirit, the Prophet Malachi wrote these words:

> And he will turn the hearts of the fathers to the children, and the hearts of the children to their fathers, lest I come and strike the earth with a curse." (Mal. 4:6)

Today the vast majority of mankind on planet Earth is fatherless. When I speak of *fatherless,* I am speaking not only of literal orphans but of orphans resulting from homes where the father was never present or was never involved in a meaningful way in the lives of his children. These children have often been damaged beyond repair by any *natural* means. Their cold-hearted feelings toward their earthly fathers have carried over to the way they view their Heavenly Father; but our Heavenly Father loves to restore those who have been broken through the effects of sin by demolishing the lies the enemy has used to call into question God's character.

As you and I journey together, we will discover the truth about whom our Father is and about whom we are in Him. We are not orphans—ones who have been *abandoned* by our Creator, but we are beloved sons and daughters. We have come into a kingdom, our eternal home, where the King is our Father. We are members of a family in which we have a loving Father who is happy to walk with us day by day, moment by moment—partnering with us for our success.

As you progress through the pages of this book, you will discover that God isn't angry with you and that He is not taken aback when you stumble. His love for you is unconditional, and you are always welcome in His presence.

It is not because of something you have done, but because of what He did for you at the Cross. You can enter into the very throne room of heaven with absolute confidence that He always has time for you and cares about the smallest, most intimate details of your life.

It is actually His invitation. Father is inviting you and me to experience eternity now. That was Jesus' prayer in John 17:3 "And this is eternal life that they might know [emphasis mine] You..." When you and I enter into this intimate relationship with our Father, understanding our position in Him, we will be able to become all that He has created us to be

The invitation is to *all* who will come, and I hope you will join me. It is an adventure that is challenging, fun, and life-giving—not only for each of you on the journey, but for all of those you will encounter along the way. As you read, take time to meditate upon the revelations of His nature and character that you might not have previously encountered. I encourage you to ask the Holy Spirit to walk with you as you peruse the following pages and to reveal the Father's true nature and character, not only to your mind but to your heart.

CHAPTER 1

HOW THE JOURNEY BEGAN

It all began in a beautiful garden where God created a man and a woman in His own image. The Garden of Eden was flawless, neither spoiled by weeds nor riddled by insects. All of the animals residing there were under the dominion of the man and woman named Adam and Eve; life was perfect.

God had told them that they could eat the fruit of every tree in the garden *except for* the tree of the knowledge of good and evil. If they ate of that tree, they would surely die.

In the garden was a serpent, identified in Revelation 12:9 as Satan himself. The serpent confronted Eve about the tree of the knowledge of good and evil and called into question God's integrity about what He had said. Slyly, he tells her, "You aren't going to die! If you eat this fruit, you will be equal to God, knowing good and evil—you will become very wise." In that moment of deception, Satan began to plant in Eve's mind a seed of distrust in the Father God.

Beguiled by the serpent, Eve not only ate the fruit of the tree of the knowledge of good and evil but shared it with her husband as well, and the Fall of man occurred. Immediately, they realized they were naked; so they covered themselves with fig leaves.

When God came to the garden later to spend time with His children, they hid from Him among the trees. I believe that it was with great sorrow that the Father did what He had to do next. Much as He loved His children and enjoyed His time with them there, He could no longer leave them in the garden—for to eat of the tree of life would allow them to live forever in their now-fallen state. As a consequence of their disobedience, God had to remove them from the beautiful garden, forever.

Outside of the garden, the enemy came again to them with the lie, "I told you He wasn't trustworthy. Now He has abandoned you—you are an orphan."

From that one act of disobedience in the garden, all of sin was ushered in. Evil reigned and ruled in the hearts of all mankind, and everyone thereafter was born into sin.

But God had a plan to rescue men from their sinful ways.

One night, expressing His servant heart, Jesus the Son of God knelt and washed the feet of His creation—twelve of His chosen disciples—and He ministered to them about life. Afterwards, He went out into another garden, the Garden of Gethsemane, and wrestled for many hours in prayer as He struggled with what He must face. For the Father had chosen Him, His only begotten Son, to become the pure and spotless sacrifice for the sin of man, thereby making a way for man to come back into relationship with Him—a way to be saved from sin and receive eternal life.

Betrayed by one of His disciples, Jesus was taken from the garden and beaten, suffering excruciating pain on behalf of all mankind as He hung on a cross—a shameful death for the entire world to see.

There was yet another garden in this story of the Fall and redemption of man. It had been three days since Jesus' crucifixion. His body had been wrapped in cloths and laid in a tomb sealed by a very large rock. Mary came to the garden to mourn the loss of her beloved Jesus. However, when she got there, she found the stone rolled away and the body of Jesus gone. Turning away, she began to weep. Through her tears, she saw one who she thought was the gardener, and asked him what had been done with Jesus' body.

Then she heard a voice call her name, *"Mary!"* And in that garden, Jesus appeared to her. Man had fallen in a garden, but now the Resurrection and the Life stood before her, and all that had been lost in that first garden was regained.

Mankind was still born into sin, but now a way of escape was made—a Savior waiting to rescue them and bring them back into the Father's loving arms.

Down through the ages, Satan has set out to destroy the works of God. The enemy of our souls has one goal in mind—to steal what is ours, destroying who we were created to be as beloved sons and daughters of God

Adam and Eve had acquired an orphan spirit when they were removed from the garden as the enemy whispered to them, "I told you that you couldn't trust Him. See, now He's abandoned you!" From that point on, they *felt* like orphans. Before Christ came, each one of us bore the DNA of Adam and Eve. As a result, each one of us has been influenced by that orphan spirit. When this spirit expresses itself in our lives, that *feeling of abandonment* attempts to take control of our thinking.

My Testimony

I was raised in a fatherless home, which is not uncommon in today's world. Though physically present, my dad had little involvement in my life. He never took the time to know me or to validate my life or my gifts. As a result, I grew up with a distorted view of my identity, not knowing what my destiny was or why I was here, and I truly didn't understand who God was.

In many ways my grandfather had been more like a father to me. I had received from him the nurturing and love that I desperately desired and wasn't receiving from my own father. However, when my grandfather died, a door was opened for the spirit of abandonment to be ushered into my young life. I was five years old, and this traumatic event was the gateway Satan used to get a foothold in my life, causing a happy little boy to shut down and stop dreaming and laughing. Insecurity and insignificance took control of my life.

These feelings increased as I grew and those closest to me spoke hurtful words, supporting the lies of the enemy. Those lies diminished my assessment of who I was destined to be and the purpose for which I was created. No longer a happy, secure little boy, I was filled with a sense of worthlessness and despair.

Raised in an environment where I never felt safe, my own dreams and callings faded; dreams and creativity are incubated in a safe and secure environment. I began to believe that my purpose was to be who others said I was, and then, perhaps by adapting to the desires of others, I could receive acceptance and affirmation.

One of the tremendous privileges a father has is to discover the gifts and talents in his children and to call them into their destiny, gently leading and encouraging them as they grow into the man or woman God has created them to be. Because I lacked this from my own father, I wandered through my teen years and on into my early twenties, still trying to discover who I was. I constantly compared myself with others. My father was very old before I ever heard him tell me that he was sorry or that he loved me and was proud of me. Because of his lack of fathering, I vowed in my heart that I would never be like my earthly father.

I longed in my heart for a real father, one who would nurture and value me. This desire sent me on a "journey" with questions that only God could answer. I had felt disqualified for years as I was growing up. Raised in a dysfunctional family, I was constantly compared with my sister. Over and over again I heard, "Why can't you be like your sister?" until I began to feel inferior to her.

Some may have thought of me as a late bloomer. I preferred to be outside discovering the adventures of a new day rather than sitting in a classroom or doing homework. This was just who I was; as a result, I was always behind in my schoolwork and, of course, my grades suffered for it. Not only did I feel inferior to my very intelligent and gifted sister, but I began to compare myself with others and believe that I just didn't have what it took to be successful in school. I just couldn't measure up to the expectations that people around me held.

These feelings carried over into the church we attended when I was a child. The church believed in "election": that some are elected to be saved and some aren't. I decided that I must be one that wasn't "elect" since I saw myself as the black sheep of the family. But when I was around 11 years old, our church took a group of us to Deland, Florida, to hear Billy Graham, and hope was awakened in my heart.

At the end of his sermon, an invitation was issued to come and receive Jesus as Lord and Savior. Greatly moved, I began to make my way to the front along with countless others, but one of the men in our group stopped me and told me the bus was leaving and we had to go.

….He has put eternity in their hearts… (Eccl. 3:11)

God has placed in each of us a desire to encounter and be encountered, to know and be known by our Creator.

That small seed of desire within me wanted so badly to find root and grow. It was watered by the Word that day and struggled to break forth, but it wasn't to be. I left that day with the desire still unfulfilled.

My heart was restless until one night 16 years later. In 1976, the Father encountered me with the revelation of the Cross. I was at home, reading the wonderful message that Jesus personally took my sins in His body on the Cross, and if I desired, I could receive Him as Lord and Savior. The Word said that not only would my sins be forgiven, but I would be given eternal life. God revealed to me that the story of the Cross wasn't just about a man who died for the sins of the world—which He did—but that it was for me, personally. My heart leaped within me, and immediately, I was on my knees beside my bed confessing my sins to God, asking for His forgiveness, and receiving Jesus into my heart. That moment is one I will never forget—it will be with me forever. I awoke the next morning with such peace. I was overjoyed. It felt as if the weight of the world had been lifted off of my back. I had come home; it was like coming home from a distant country.

All of life is a coming home. Salesmen, secretaries, coal miners, beekeepers, sword swallowers, all of us. All the restless hearts of the world, all trying to find a way home.[1]

From that point on, I began an incredible journey into the Father's heart, discovering who He is and who I am in Him. I had now become fully qualified as His beloved son. I must confess that at times I still exhibited the characteristics of an orphan—I knew beyond the shadow of a doubt that I was born again, but I still wasn't completely free from the great pain in my life. It has been a journey, but all along I have known the loving Father's presence. He has never been too busy to listen and never been impatient in my growth process. He has never condemned me when fears and doubts came; He only loved me, and as a result of His love and tender care, my heart has begun to heal.

Life's greatest happiness is to be convinced we are loved.[2]

In so many ways, I was rejected by my earthly father. I felt disqualified, unaccepted, insecure, and unsafe; so when I came into the church, it was with these hidden pains. Like most believers, I found it easy to receive the free gift of salvation by grace through faith in Jesus Christ. On the other hand, as I began to look at the race set before me, no matter how hard I tried, I felt that I would never be able to perform at a level that would satisfy Father God. If I were unable to meet my earthly father's expectations, how in the world could I ever hope to satisfy my Heavenly Father's?

The enemy uses such lies to keep us bound and to distort our perception of the Father. As a result of this misconception, many have come to believe that He is demanding, angry, harsh, and unfair; they think they can never satisfy Him and that He rewards us when we perform and punishes us when we fail. They think He is sitting on a throne in heaven far out of reach, mostly sad and lacking a sense of humor, haughtily watching everything we do, and just waiting for us to make a mistake.

This misrepresentation of the character of God is an absolute lie from the pit of hell. The wonderful thing that I have learned—not in my head but in my heart and by experience—is that He is eternally good. Even when we are going through great suffering, He is kind, faithful, and loving, delighting in each one of us just the way we are.

He isn't shaken when we stumble but is always by our side as we run this race of faith with Him.

Like me, many have come into the family of God, delighting in the wonder of the free gift of our salvation from the Father. We are touched by such an expression of His incredible grace towards us! But then we become influenced by the law and legalism.

Many of us have been held captive by this legalistic approach, and I am convinced it is because of the lies and wounds that have been inflicted upon us, particularly by our earthly fathers. Because of these wounds, we have misconstrued the true character of Father God. Now those same lies and wounds cause us to allow an orphan spirit to express itself outwardly through our actions and attitudes. Much like the second son in the prodigal story, our response is to perform. We discipline our lives and work hard at doing what we feel will get the Father's pleasure. All the while, we become overwhelmed by a religious yoke that has settled over us as we attempt to satisfy the works of the law.

I do believe in a disciplined life in Christ. I love spending time with the Lord in His Word and living my life in a manner that is pleasing to the Lord—not because I *have* to, but because I *want* to. It is not a burdensome thing but a joy. For years, I attempted to do outward religious things in order to move the heart of God, but all the while, I already had His undivided attention and unconditional love. It was the fear of man that drove me to do those things, and I began to react—much like the Pharisees—to that religious spirit.

I finally grew weary of living like that and decided to come into my Father's rest; to abide in Him in the fullness of His love and in the finished work of the Cross. I began to allow Him to lead me with the full knowledge that He has my best interest in mind. I am learning to enter into the freedom that Paul spoke of in his letter to the Galatians. Several years ago, I was going through some hard challenges and waking one morning, I heard the Lord say, "I am so content with you

I remember responding, "Excuse me?"

Once again I heard Him say, "I am so content with you."

I replied, "Well, I am certainly content with You."

Those simple, yet profound words have set me free to be more and more of who He created me to be. Today I do know who I am, what I am to be about, and where I am going. My journey with the Father is one of continued discovery and adventure.

Jesus said that the enemy comes to kill, steal, and destroy, and he does so through wounds, lies, fear, rejection, and shame. The enemy is continually trying to bring back shame for sins from which we have already been forgiven, attempting to make us feel guilty and disqualified.

Coming as a child, innocent and without fear, secure in the fact that He is—and will *always* be—the same, we can rest in His eternal, unconditional, and unfailing love. In every way, Jesus and our Father are One. Every attribute that we see manifested through the life of Christ is a reflection of the Father. As you read each chapter, be on the lookout for these. Herein you will find many, though certainly not all, of the attributes of our wonderful Heavenly Father.

You will also identify problems that you may have struggled with over the years as you read the testimonies of others, as well as some of the encounters that Jesus had with people during His time here on earth. These problems are frequently brought on by this orphan spirit. As we learn more about who our Father is and who we are in Him, it is my hope that you will be able to overcome the things that have hindered you from having a close, trusting relationship with our loving Father.

I invite you to join me on this journey because I know that there are so many who are fatherless and hurting in one way or another. I want you to discover what I discovered while searching for a father, and to know the freedom and joy that I have found in personally knowing my real Father. Let's begin our *Journey Into the Father's Heart.*

CHAPTER 2

IN THE BEGINNING

We can never know who or what we are until
we know at least something of what God is. [4]

John's words in John 17 coincide with this:

And this is eternal life, that they may know You, the only true
God, and Jesus Christ whom You have sent. (John 17:3)

As we make our journey, we will learn about some of
the characteristics that define the Father, but it will only
be possible to touch on a few of His many glorious attributes. There are so many that He will continue to fasci-
nate us throughout all eternity, revealing more and more
of who He is.

The prophet Jeremiah spoke thousands of years ago
revealing God's heart to His people, but God declares the
same words to us today:

"Yes, I have loved you with an everlasting love; Therefore
with loving-kindness I have drawn you. (Jer. 31:3)

"Everlasting love"—His love will never end—is who
He is. God is love! And Jesus is the sole expression of the
glory of God; He is the perfect imprint and the very image of God's nature. As we see Jesus and walk with Him
through some of His encounters with mankind, keep in
mind that Jesus and the Father are one; if we have looked

upon the face of Jesus, we have looked upon the face of the Father.

As you embrace the truth of His Word, you will also find that God is the kindest person you have ever known. He is our Creator as well as our eternal Father, and we can bring all of our dreams and all of our failures to Him without fear of condemnation or judgment. Nothing is too great or too small to bring to our Father.

Fatherhood Brings Privilege and Responsibility

Earthly fatherhood should mirror the relationship that Jesus had with His Father. Created in the Father's image, loving earthly fathers will recognize gifts in each of their children and gently encourage their growth. Like precious seeds, God has placed these gifts within them. An earthly father has been given the privilege and responsibility to help cultivate each one of these. He needs to provide a safe environment in which these seeds can grow and mature.

A loving father is in partnership with God—he has been entrusted with these priceless treasures and displays his unconditional love and approval for each child, supporting them in every way possible and helping them to become all that their Heavenly Father created them to be. He disciples them, for he knows the day will come when they must leave home and continue to walk out their destiny in God on their own. He teaches them of the love of the Father for them as expressed in the gift of His Son and leads them to a personal relationship with Jesus Christ. Through his own example—one of absolute trust in and dependency upon God—he is a loving reflection of the Heavenly Father.

In this safe environment, children are able to develop their own personal relationship with the Father, revealing their purpose and destiny. Two important foundational truths will be brought to light: first, that they are beloved children of God, and secondly, that they are fully validated and approved for who they were uniquely created to be.

As they grow and mature in an environment that has been fashioned by a loving, earthly father, they will be secure and begin to see the dreams they have in their hearts unfold and become a reality. When they experience pain, he is a refuge. Even when they fail, their father is always there to pick them up and encourage them, and if needed, carry them.

❦❦❧❦

The Derek Redmond Story

I remember watching on television as the following beautiful example of a father's love unfolded:

Having prepared all of his life for the Summer Olympics of 1992, Derek Redmond was a favorite in the 400-meter sprint. He held the world record time in that event, but had never won the gold medal despite winning all of his earlier races. In a magnificent start, he shot off of the starting blocks, but as he rounded the last turn with only 175 meters to go, he suddenly collapsed on the track with a snapped hamstring. The crowd watched in horror. Derek managed to get to his feet and hobble slowly and agonizingly toward the finish line.

As the entire stadium looked on, not knowing what to do, I saw an older man begin to make his way out of the stands. Pushing past the security guards who tried to prevent him, he ran out onto the track to Derek's side. As I watched, I saw his father wrap his arm around his son and tell him he didn't have to do this.

But Derek argued that he had to. And so the father simply replied that they would do it together. It was an unforgettable scene as his father helped Derek walk to the finish line. Afterwards, his father declared with tears in his eyes that he was the proudest father alive—even prouder of Derek than if he had won the gold medal.

Derek Redmond never did get that gold medal, but the memory lives on of his father who shared his pain and finished the race at his side. Despite being told that his athletic career was over, Derek went on to play professional basketball and rugby, and to race motorcycles—encouraged by his father. Derek also became a motivational speaker to encourage others, no doubt inspired by his father's example.

What an incredible victory and what a fantastic picture of a loving father! Each one of us was created to be loved and to love, to be overcomers, victorious even in the midst of great challenges.

The Ultimate Carpenter—Shaping the Lives of His Sons and Daughters

In the Gospels, we read the great example of a loving relationship between a father and His Son. Jesus was born in a stable with a manger for His bed; though from humble beginnings, He was raised in a loving environment. He learned firsthand what it is like to grow up in a loving home with an earthly father and mother. As a little boy, Jesus would go with Joseph to his workshop. There He watched as His earthly father crafted all kinds of useful items out of wood. I can see Joseph turn to Jesus and say, "Watch, my son; see how I sort through the woodpile in order to select the finest pieces for the table I am making. It needs to be straight and strong in order to last for many years to come. The table will be where the family will meet for meals having many wonderful conversations as they sit together enjoying fellowship with one another." Then one day, Joseph had Jesus build a table all by Himself.

It was in this safe environment that Jesus discovered who He was and what His destiny was. He would become the Ultimate Carpenter, crafting and shaping men and women's lives into what they were meant to be. Through this loving relationship with Joseph, His earthly father, Jesus would learn to hear and see His Heavenly Father, to only speak what He heard the Father speak and only do what He saw Him do.

Jesus grew and developed from a baby into a little boy, into a teenager, and then into a man. When He was twelve years old, His parents took Him to Jerusalem to celebrate the Passover. At the end of the days of observance, His parents started out on their journey home, not realizing that Jesus had stayed behind. Returning to Jerusalem in search of Him, they found Him in the temple.

Now so it was that after three days they found Him in the temple, sitting in the midst of the teachers, both listening to them and asking them questions. And all who heard Him were astonished at His understanding and answers. So when they saw Him, they were amazed; and His mother said to Him, "Son, why have You done this to us? Look, Your father and I have sought You anxiously."

And He said to them, "Why did you seek Me? Did you not know that I must be about My Father's business?" But they did not understand the statement which He spoke to them. Then He went down with them and came to Nazareth, and was subject to them, but His mother kept all these things in her heart. And Jesus increased in wisdom and stature, and in favor with God and men. (Luke 2:46-52)

At the age of twelve, Jesus' heart was so impassioned with love for His Father and for His Father's will that He desired "to be about My Father's business." Yet willingly, He returned to Nazareth, and for the next eighteen years, He grew in wisdom and stature and in favor with God and men.

In John's Gospel, we read:

> *In the beginning was the Word, and the Word was with God, and the Word was God. He was in the beginning with God. (John 1:1-2)*

Jesus has eternally been the Son of God. His relationship with His Father is the ultimate example of a loving father and son. To understand more fully their eternal relationship, look at the word *with* in the previous text—it means "to be turned face-to-face." There is no deeper or more intimate relationship that can be expressed, where nothing is hidden; it is fully vulnerable.

The story that we read in Luke seems to suddenly stop at the age of twelve, but it begins again when Jesus is thirty years old—eighteen years had passed. Patiently, He had submitted to His earthly mother and father, but the day came when it was the Father's time to reveal His Son. Jesus began a journey and calling that impacted the entire world—not just in His generation but forever.

He knew that one day He would be nailed to a cross, bearing the sins of the world. What was it that sustained Him in the years ahead as He faced incredible rejection and criticism?

> *When He had been baptized, Jesus came up immediately from the water; and behold, the heavens were opened to Him, and He saw the Spirit of God descending like a dove and alighting upon Him. And suddenly a voice came from heaven, saying, "This is My beloved Son, in whom I am well pleased." (Matt. 3:16-17)*

These words *"My beloved Son, in whom I am well pleased"* are the most significant words that a child can ever hear from a loving father. They engender wellbeing and confidence in the heart of a child. They provide a foundation upon which children can build their lives and express their gifts and talents to the fullest.

The Father's Heart From the Beginning

> *Then God said, "Let Us make man in Our image, according to Our likeness;…(Gen. 1:26)*
>
> *And the Lord God formed man of the dust of the ground, and breathed into his nostrils the breath of life; and man became a living being. (Gen. 2: 7)*

The story of Creation is a continual reminder to us of who our Heavenly Father is and what He is like. Hebrews tells us that God spoke into the void and that which was not emerged.

> *"…the worlds were framed by the word of God, so that the things which are seen were not made of things which are visible" (Heb. 11:3).*
>
> *"And God saw everything that He had made, and indeed it was very good." (Gen. 1:31)*

Everything God makes is good. The last thing God created was man. Instead of speaking man into existence, He reached down into the earth, and with His own hands fashioned man, breathing the breath of life into him. Made in His image and given great dignity and honor, man would have everything he required. God placed within him gifts of creativity and unlimited ability to accomplish all that He had destined for him (see Gen. 1:28).

Formed in God's image, mankind was to be a complete reflection of His very nature and character. All of creation was for God's good pleasure, but this part of His creation was His family—sons and daughters with whom He would fellowship and share His heart.

In preparation for mankind's arrival, God fashioned a garden; a place where He would meet with them and enjoy their presence. It was a home of incredible beauty, representing an outward expression of His infinite love and care for them.

God commanded all of the animals He had created to pass before Adam, and He gave Adam the privilege of naming each one (Gen. 2:19-20). By this act, God was inviting Adam into a partnership with Himself as a co-regent in ruling and reigning over all He had created (Gen. 1:28), and this command given to mankind has never been altered. Through the sons and daughters God created, He wants to bring the reality of His kingdom to earth and to subdue and have dominion over His created order.

But rebellion lurked in the midst of the seemingly peaceful environment of the beautiful garden God had created.

CHAPTER 3

HE HAS ABANDONED YOU

Why do so many people struggle with relating to the Father? Why do they find it hard to trust Him and turn to Him?

At the beginning of our journey, we need to be fully aware that to establish an intimate relationship, it is imperative to build it on absolute trust, vulnerability, and transparency. Each of these is the bedrock upon which a lasting relationship is built.

I have often wondered, why two trees? Scripture tells us there were two trees in the middle of the Garden of Eden; one of them, Adam and Eve were commanded not to eat from—the tree of knowledge of good and evil. God gave them a *choice* whether or not to freely love and trust Him. To do otherwise would have been to create human beings that were androids—not beloved sons and daughters—programmed to do exactly what the "Programmer" designed them to be.

From the very beginning of time, the Father's original plan was for man to:

"Be fruitful and multiply; fill the earth and subdue it; have dominion over the fish of the sea, over the birds of the air, and over every living thing that moves on the earth." (Gen. 1:28)

Made in His image, man would partner with Him in establishing and advancing the kingdom of God and His will on the earth. In order to subdue and have dominion, there must be someone or something to subdue. So we discover that in the garden was a serpent that *"was more cunning than any beast of the field which the Lord God had made."* God had allowed Satan, man's archenemy, to be present on the earth at the time of the creation of man for the specific purpose of preparing His sons and daughters to rule and reign with Him.

God could have spoken one word and Satan would have been annihilated—yet, He chose not to. It is important to understand that God was present with Adam and Eve at all times. When the serpent came to them, they could have called on God for help, even in the midst of the temptation, and He would have helped them; but sadly, they did not.

Since Adam's fall we have come to picture God not as a loving Father inviting us to trust Him, but an exacting sovereign who must be appeased.[5]

Some today believe that God is like a great watchmaker who created a clock and then left it to its own devices. This is a tremendous distortion of what a loving and caring father is. Throughout the ages, this misconception has been used by the enemy to demean the true nature and character of God.

In the account in Genesis, we see that the Father came to walk with His children in the garden in the cool of the day. What good father would not want to be with his beloved child—his most precious possession? As we journey, we must continually remind ourselves of this truth—our Father wants to be with us and have a loving relationship with each of us. To think otherwise would be to allow the enemy to distort the glory and majesty of our loving Father.

Satan Comes to Adam and Eve in the Garden

Satan hated mankind. Man would be his greatest nemesis. According to Scripture, Lucifer (or Satan) was the most beautiful angel God had created, and his position in heaven was above all the other angels. Like mankind, he had been given a free will, and by his own choice had disobeyed God in an attempt to become greater than God. As a result, God threw him out of heaven to the earth. (See Isaiah 14:12-15 and Ezekiel 28:15.)

On the earth, Satan watched as God formed and fashioned man with His own hands. Made in God's own image, man was the pinnacle of His creation. As God placed man in the amazing paradise of Eden, Satan heard God give Adam and Eve the command to subdue and have dominion over all He had created … including Satan. God not only gave them the command, but He gave them the authority and power to carry out His command.

Not only had Satan lost his position and authority in heaven, but now he saw himself being usurped by these lumps of clay. He was livid with jealousy. He hated God and he hated mankind. From that moment, Satan would begin to devise a plan to thwart the purposes of God. As Adam and Eve were confronted with the enemy's temptation—ending in their fall and separation from God—God implemented His own plan. *His* great plan was one that would defeat Satan by making available to all mankind the means by which they could be reconciled to God.

When Satan asked Eve, *"Has God indeed said, 'You shall not eat of every tree of the garden?'"* he was accusing God of not telling Eve the truth—it was not an obvious lie, but rather, a subtle one; he was setting a trap with the intent to cast doubt in Eve's mind regarding the integrity of God. Eve had a *choice*—agree with the lie, thereby empowering it; or reflect on the truth of her experience with the Lord.

Eve chose to trust Satan's deception and lies rather than her Father. She reached out and took the fruit and ate. Falling for the lie of the enemy, she questioned the goodness of God and was deceived.

Then, she offered the fruit to her husband and he also bought into the lie of Satan. Instead of Adam and Eve's eyes being opened, their spiritual vision was distorted, and their intimate relationship with their Creator was broken. That day brought spiritual death—and ultimately their physical death.

Because of their disobedience, Adam and Eve lost their spiritual acuity and their fellowship with God. They relinquished their God-given rule and authority over the earth to Satan. The glory of God that had covered them was removed, and they realized that they were naked. Emotions such as they had never experienced before— fear and shame—overwhelmed them; and they ran and hid from God.

> Then the eyes of both of them were opened, and they knew that they were naked; and they sewed fig leaves together and made themselves coverings. And they heard the sound of the Lord God walking in the garden in the cool of the day, and Adam and his wife hid themselves from the presence of the Lord God among the trees of the garden. Then the Lord God called to Adam and said to him, "Where are you?" So he said, "I heard Your voice in the garden, and I was afraid because I was naked; and I hid myself."
>
> And He said, "Who told you that you were naked? Have you eaten from the tree of which I commanded you that you should not eat?"

Then the man said, "The woman whom You gave to be with me, she gave me of the tree, and I ate."

And the Lord God said to the woman, "What is this you have done?"

The woman said, "The serpent deceived me, and I ate."

So the Lord God said to the serpent: "Because you have done this, you are cursed more than all cattle, And more than every beast of the field; On your belly you shall go, and you shall eat dust all the days of your life. And I will put enmity between you and the woman, And between your seed and her Seed; He shall bruise your head, And you shall bruise His heel." (Gen. 3:7-15)

Hidden in these words was a promise! It was God's plan to reconcile man to Himself, *"He shall bruise your head, and you shall bruise His heel."* God's plan of redemption, though a mystery to Adam and Eve at that time, was a revelation of His unconditional love. In His perfect timing, the mystery would unfold, fully accomplishing His will.

Thousands of years later, there was another garden; one that contained a tomb—the tomb where the Son of God's body had been laid. But on the third day as the women came to the tomb, they discovered that the stone which covered the entrance to the tomb had been removed. Looking inside, they discovered the body of Jesus was missing. As the others left, Mary Magdalene fell behind, weeping uncontrollably. Not only had the One she loved died, but now His body had been stolen.

But Mary stood outside by the tomb weeping, and as she wept she stooped down and looked into the tomb. And she saw two angels in white sitting, one at the head and the other at the feet, where the body of Jesus had lain. Then they said to her, "Woman, why are you weeping?"

She said to them, "Because they have taken away my Lord, and I do not know where they have laid Him."

Now when she had said this, she turned around and saw Jesus standing there, and did not know that it was Jesus. Jesus said to her, "Woman, why are you weeping? Whom are you seeking?"

She, supposing Him to be the gardener, said to Him, "Sir, if You have carried Him away, tell me where You have laid Him, and I will take Him away."

Jesus said to her, "Mary!"

She turned and said to Him, "Rabboni!" (which is to say, Teacher).

Jesus said to her, "Do not cling to Me, for I have not yet ascended to My Father; but go to My brethren and say to them, 'I am ascending to My Father and your Father, and to My God and your God.'" (John 20:11-17)

The promise that God had first given in a garden found its completion in another garden thousands of years later.

Many times we read so quickly through events in the Bible that we miss the heart of the message being conveyed. So for a moment, let's stop and consider what the Holy Spirit is revealing to us. When we read about the Fall in the garden, we find that Eve was the one who was tempted and disobeyed first, but that gave no excuse for men—Adam followed suit. Look at the incredible love of the Father as He redeems this incident that started with a woman. I don't believe it was a coincidence that the others left the garden tomb on the Resurrection morning, and Mary was alone in the garden. The Fall of mankind began in a garden, with a woman first, and the restoration of mankind to the Father would be initiated in a garden, with a woman first.

Can you see this as you read this story? Here, unrecognized by Mary, is the risen Author of Life standing before her, just as He stood with Adam and Eve in the Garden. *"Woman, why are you weeping?"* He asks Mary. Through her pain and tears, she doesn't recognize His voice. Then, He speaks her name, *"Mary!"* Notice how incredibly intimate God is as He calls her by name. This is how He is with His sons and daughters.

Now, as she recognizes who He is, Mary turns and reaches out to Him, but Jesus tells her not to hold onto Him. *"… I am ascending to My Father and your Father …"* In the first garden, Eve knew the pain of separation from her loving Father. Now, thousands of years later in another garden, another woman experiences the incredible joy of reunion with her loving Heavenly Father—our Father. To me, this is one of the most incredible displays of the infinite love of our Father and what He is *really* like—not how He has been represented by the enemy.

The Problem Is Our Eyesight

Turning our attention back to the story in the Garden of Eden, once again we hear the Father speaking to Adam and Eve, pronouncing over them the cost of their disobedience

As a father and grandfather, I can only imagine the hurt and pain He must have felt as He spoke those words over his son and daughter. Adam and Eve suffered the penalty for their sins, and we, their descendants, not only inherited their sinful nature but we have also been blinded to the truth of who our Heavenly Father truly is and how He sees us. All this is changed, however, for everyone who by faith receives Jesus Christ as Lord and Savior and in so doing, receives His heredity and all the benefits of the Father's loving plan of redemption.

*The moral miracle of Redemption is that God can put into me
a new disposition (nature) whereby I can live a totally new life.
When I reach the frontier of need and know my limitations,
Jesus says – "Blessed are you."[6]*

Returning again to Adam and Eve in Genesis 3, we see the Father performing a prophetic act. He killed an innocent animal, pouring out its blood and taking its skin as a covering for the guilty pair. There had never been death in all of His creation; yet, now as an act of love, God would kill an innocent animal, spilling its blood on the very ground from which He had formed Adam.

> "...for Adam and his wife the Lord God made tunics of skin, and clothed them" (vs. 21).

> ...and without the shedding of blood there is neither release from sin and its guilt nor the remission of the due and merited punishment for sins. (Heb. 9:22 AMP)

In fear and shame, they had covered themselves with fig leaves—their own works—much like many religious people do today in their attempts to impress God. It was beyond Satan's understanding that God gazed down the corridor of time seeing His own Son, His sacrificial Lamb, "...the Lamb slain from the foundation of the world" (Rev. 13:8), being slain for the sins of the world. He saw His own priceless and precious blood spilled on a dusty hill in Jerusalem for the sins of the world.

At the same moment that His Son bowed His head in death, the veil in the temple that had separated man from God was torn in two from top to bottom. This was symbolic of the Father reaching down to us, allowing us to come back into relationship with Him through Jesus.

But God, who is rich in mercy, because of His great love with which He loved us, even when we were dead in trespasses, made us alive together with Christ (by grace you have been saved)… (Eph. 2:4)

But God demonstrates His own love toward us, in that while we were still sinners, Christ died for us." (Rom. 5:8)

It is important to lay this foundation of truth in the beginning of our journey because through the light of truth, darkness is driven out of our hearts. We can never forget that forgiveness, redemption, and restoration are provided through the cost of the Cross as well as God bringing us back into relationship with Him.

In the Father's final act of love that day, He placed

Once you realize all that it cost God to forgive you, you will be held as in a vise, constrained by the love of God.[7]

Adam and Eve outside of the garden, for He knew that if they ate of the tree of life they would live eternally in their fallen state, separated from Him.

Then the Lord God said, "Behold, the man has become like one of Us, to know good and evil. And now, lest he put out his hand and take also of the tree of life, and eat, and live forever"— therefore the Lord God sent him out of the garden of Eden to till the ground from which he was taken. So He drove out the man; and He placed cherubim at the east of the garden of Eden, and a flaming sword which turned every way, to guard the way to the tree of life. (Gen. 3:22-24)

So they were outside of the garden and alone—or so they thought—and the enemy's ferocious lies echoed in their ears, "See how God has abandoned you? Now you are alone; you are an orphan!"

CHAPTER 4

WHAT HINDERS OUR RELATIONSHIP WITH THE FATHER?

"If you had known Me, you would have known My Father also; and from now on you know Him and have seen Him."

Philip said to Him, "Lord, show us the Father, and it is sufficient for us."

Jesus said to him, "Have I been with you so long, and yet you have not known Me, Philip? He who has seen Me has seen the Father; so how can you say, 'Show us the Father'? Do you not believe that I am in the Father, and the Father in Me? The words that I speak to you I do not speak on My own authority; but the Father who dwells in Me does the works. (John 14:7-10)

It was the night of Jesus' betrayal. The disciples had been with Him for over three years. They had lived in His presence, followed Him, ministered with Him, and had been taught by Him. Jesus was revealing the Father to them. And yet, right after clearly telling the disciples that if they knew Him, they would know the Father also, Philip asked Him to show them the Father; that would be good enough for them. Jesus' answer was that they should have already seen the Father in Him.

Our first parents in the garden passed down their poor spiritual eyesight, and we have inherited it. Eve thought it sounded good when the enemy declared that if she ate of the tree of life, her eyes would be opened and she would become as wise as God. Instead, when the first couple ate the forbidden fruit, their vision became distorted, impacting the way they viewed their Heavenly Father and in turn, their relationship with Him. Because of the Fall of man, that imperfect vision was passed down to all mankind.

When Adam and Eve heard God's voice in the garden, they were afraid because they were naked (Gen. 3:10) so they hid themselves. Consequently, an orphan spirit was introduced to all of mankind. Fear, shame, insecurity, isolation, and other personality traits opposite to the Father's character were cultivated and nurtured by lies and wounds inflicted upon them and all mankind. As God removed the man and woman from the garden in order to protect them from eternal separation from God, Satan's lying accusation that God had abandoned them attached itself to mankind and passed down through the ages so that all men and women would see themselves as orphans! Every human being ever born has inherited the spiritual DNA of this orphan spirit.

Recognized by specific characteristics, the orphan is driven particularly by a spirit of fear of man. Many become performers—laboring to win man's approval by their actions and achievements—and are bathed in insecurity. They are generally perfectionists with a slave mentality, possessing critical and judgmental personalities. Perhaps the strongest characteristic they harbor is shame.

The greatest fear that the enemy has is that you and I might come to the revelation of who we truly are in the eyes of God and find hope of a loving Father. Therefore, he fights hard to see that our hearts are wounded, assaulted with lies, rejected, disqualified and filled with despair—leaving us feeling fatherless.

A bruised reed He will not break, And smoking flax He will not quench; He will bring forth justice for truth. (Is. 42:3)

The word *bruised* means "to be broken, to be crushed; to be crushed to pieces." The bruised reed has lost its strength, its stability, and its soundness. For a person, this means they have lost their hope. This verse refers to God's Servant, His Elect One in whom God delights. And God is saying through the prophet Isaiah that His Son, empowered by the Holy Spirit, will come bringing hope and encouragement to the weak and hurting. Today, blinded to the truth, many Christians are struggling to believe that they are God's beloved sons and daughters; they have agreed with the lies of the enemy.

I shared previously that several years ago as I was awakening, I heard the Lord say to me, "I am so content with you." These words came at a time when I was struggling with my own identity. My self-image was being influenced by the same orphan spirit that attacks so many of us. It had caused me to compare myself with others who I thought were more mature and more spiritual. It was robbing me of my joy and relationship with the Father. Subtly influenced by the enemy, I was being deceived into believing that I wasn't performing well enough to be acceptable before God.

I found myself becoming like those that the Apostle Paul was writing to in his letter to the Galatians. *"O foolish Galatians, who has bewitched you…?" (Gal. 3:1).* They had returned to the law, setting aside the grace of God by which they had been saved! As the Father repeated those words to me, "I am so content with you," and I responded that I was content with Him as well, the lie that was being fed to me evaporated. Light drove out the darkness and truth exposed the lie.

The letter that Paul wrote to the Ephesians contains truths that extend to you and me as well.

> ...*just as He chose us in Him before the foundation of the world, that we should be holy and without blame before Him in love, having predestined us to adoption as sons by Jesus Christ to Himself, according to the good pleasure of His will...* (Eph. 1:4-5)

When a family adopts a child, they spend countless hours and incredible amounts of money to choose one who isn't even naturally their own. Yet out of love they choose to embrace and bring the child into their family with all the rights and privileges that a naturally-born child would have.

Consider what our Heavenly Father has done for you and me and the incalculable cost he expended in order to adopt us into His family. You and I were created and destined to be His children *"...chosen in Him before the foundation of the world...according to the good pleasure of His will."* As you read down through Eph. 1:3-14, the Word tells us that we have been *"accepted in the Beloved"* which means to be fully accepted into the household of the Father. We have *"obtained an inheritance"* in Him (Christ) having been redeemed by His blood, and we have been *"sealed with the Holy Spirit of promise."* That seal is the *"guarantee of our inheritance."*

As we continue our journey, we must allow the light of the truth of His Word to dispel the lies that have been spoken over us and to break our agreement with those lies. Along the way, take time to allow the Holy Spirit to reveal His truth to you, for Jesus said, *"You will know the truth and the truth will set you free"* (John 8:32).

For most of us, our perception of the Father originated out of our relationship or lack of relationship with our earthly fathers. This relationship created a lens in our hearts through which we perceive the Father, also affecting how we believe He sees us.

Perfectionism

ॐ᪳ॐ᪳

Anne's Testimony
(The name has been changed to protect her privacy.)

I thought that if I wanted approval and love from my parents, I had to work hard and perform well with good grades…

After I got saved, my impression of the Heavenly Father was that of a strict disciplinarian, One who would punish me if I disobeyed Him, and I needed to perform well in order to gain more love, approval, and favor from Him.

ॐ᪳ॐ᪳

This young woman had been led to believe that her Heavenly Father was just like her earthly father. In order to get His approval, she needed to perform. This is an example of an orphan spirit. It was nurtured by the lies of the enemy that were inflicted upon her as a young girl.

Without a revelation of the Father's heart, His nature and character, we become workers for God instead of beloved sons and daughters. But some think it is pointless to try—if they cannot please their own fathers, how can they please the God of the universe?

> *Will the Lord be pleased with thousands of rams, ten thousand rivers of oil? Shall I give my firstborn for my transgression, the fruit of my body for the sin of my soul? (Mic. 6:7*

God's favor never rests on what I can give Him, but on what He has already given me through the Cross!

Orphan or Beloved Son or Daughter

There is in the heart of every believer a tension of whether he is an orphan or a beloved son or daughter.

Susan's Testimony

(The name has been changed to protect her privacy.

When I was a child, there was no doubt in my mind that I was loved and valued by both of my parents. In fact, my dad even quit a demanding job because he knew he wasn't spending enough time with my older sister and me. He made a point to take us on "daddy-daughter dates" every few weeks. We usually went to an old-fashioned drugstore where they sold the best ice cream and milkshakes I can remember....

The only thing that seemed to challenge our family's loving dynamic was my father's passive-aggressive tendencies. His reactions to my rule-breaking were often unpredictable, and his confrontations with my mother were verbally explosive. They only happened once or twice a year, but when they did, a litany of her offenses from months past would pour out in his arguments against her. They would yell and argue for a couple of hours, and then, miraculously, everything was better the next day when a vase of flowers showed up on the kitchen table.

My relationship with Jesus began at age fifteen, but my safe, loving world was abruptly shattered at seventeen: my dad asked my mom for a divorce … he moved to another state and the divorce was finalized about a year later. He remarried about seven months after that. I harbored intense anger toward my dad and refused to forgive him for several years. My relationship with God was profoundly impacted by my unhealthy relationship with my dad: I was unable to call God by the name "Father," I refused to trust Him with relationships with men, and I simply could not believe that I could someday have a healthy marriage.

Fortunately, I had some wise mentors during these difficult years who refused to let me stay in a place of bitterness and unforgiveness. I was meeting with one of these mentors at the beginning of a college semester when she boldly declared, "I believe you are going to be able to call God 'Father' by the end of this month." I laughed at her, incredulous: The date was August 30. I wanted nothing to do with her crazy, faith-filled idea, but she convinced me to pray with her. She made me pray first, and the essential message of my prayers was, "God, I don't believe you can do this." Then she began to pray, and one of the most miraculous experiences of my life began to unfold.

I don't recall a word my friend was praying, because I was immediately aware of an attack on my body. In my mind's eye, it was as if I could see and feel dozens of red-hot darts hurtling toward my body. (I later concluded that these were the fiery darts of the enemy.) At the same time, I was aware of a large bubble that seemed to originate from my friend's body, but it extended around my body, as well. (I later decided that this must have been her shield of faith, protecting us both.) As she continued to pray, the attack became more and more intense. Finally, I could endure it no longer, and a voice that seemed to come from deep in my gut rose out of my mouth and said, "Father, make them go away!" Immediately, the fiery darts retreated, and I was filled with peace, joy, and trust in a loving Father. I began praying again, voicing my trust in Him and my confidence that He would do good things in all of my relationships with men. Up to this day, my favorite name to call God by is "Father."

---

*Trying to compensate God for His mercy will be as futile as trying
to earn it, and it will always leave me guessing
whether He loves me, or He loves me not.*[8]

After this supernatural experience, I was able to freely and lovingly forgive my dad, though I did have to make it a daily discipline to choose to forgive him. Our relationship has been repaired and renewed in miraculous ways, though it still has its difficulties. In many ways, my dad has abdicated the role of father. I think he feels that he has hurt me too deeply to continue doing the things that good dads should do: take authority in his child's life, provide guidance and advice, and provide truthful but gentle correction. As a result, I have had to turn to God the Father to fill this role in my life. And He faithfully does, in very practical ways.

For example, I have had to rely on the Father to teach me how to establish healthy boundaries in my relationships. Many children can rely on their parents to teach them when to say "yes" or "no" to the demands of others. Instead, I have had to listen to the guidance of my Heavenly Father to know what decisions are healthy for me—physically, spiritually, and emotionally. My learning curve in this area was not always quick or easy, but I have come to be sensitive to the promptings of the Holy Spirit. Many times, I can sense right away if a decision will be beneficial or not … I listen for the nudging of my Father's heart, and often, I know what He is prompting me to do. My mother has commented that my sense of boundaries—and my decision-making in general—are not something she or my dad taught me. She has remarked that I respond to difficult situations with the maturity of a person much older than myself. I have simply told her that I have learned these life skills directly from the best parent: God Himself.

If I had remained in a place of bitterness and unforgiveness, and if I had not allowed the Lord to parent me when my earthly father stepped out of his parenting role, I would not be the maturing, healthy person I am today. I have a stable job that I love, and I am growing as a professional. I have a supportive church and community of friends. I continue to find loving, truthful, and patient ways of relating with my family members…. I love my dad very much, but I am also able to make sure that his flaws do not influence me in unhealthy ways. I rely, instead, on the perfect parenting of my wise, creative, Heavenly Father.

এঁএঁৼঁএঁ

The Prodigal Son

One day Jesus told a story about a prodigal son and his elder brother. The younger brother asked for his inheritance, so the father divided his livelihood between the two sons. The younger son left and went to a far country where he foolishly squandered all that he had. When famine arose in that country, he found himself so desperate for food he would gladly have eaten with the pigs that he was feeding, but no one offered him anything. Finally, he came to his senses and realized that his father's servants received better care than he was getting—they were always fed. So he decided to go back and repent before his father, declaring that he had sinned and was not worthy to be his son, but that he would become one of the servants, if his father would just take him back.

When his father saw him coming, still a long distance away, he had compassion and ran to him and hugged and kissed his son. The son began his prepared speech but the father didn't even let him finish. He commanded the servants to bring the best robe and a ring for his finger and sandals for his feet. He also commanded that they kill the fatted calf. *"'Let us eat and be merry; for this my son was dead and is alive again; he was lost and is found.'"* And they began to celebrate his beloved son's return.

The older brother coming in from the field drew near to the house and heard a big celebration with music and dancing. He called one of the servants to find out what was going on and was told *"'Your brother has come and because he has received him safe and sound, your father has killed the fatted calf.'"* The elder son was irate and refused to go into the celebration; his father came out and pleaded with him to come join them

Angrily, the son said, "You know I have been serving you for many years. I've never gone against you even once! And you have never even given me a young goat to make merry with my friends. But as soon as this son of yours returned after wasting his whole inheritance—your *livelihood*—on harlots, you killed the fatted calf for him!" I can just hear the older son's accusing tone and see the anger flashing from his eyes.

The father gently replied to him, *"'Son, you are always with me, and all that I have is yours. It was right that we should make merry and be glad, for your brother was dead and is alive again, and was lost and is found'"* (Luke 15:11-32). Each of these sons is expressing an orphan personality. In this case it doesn't appear that the orphan spirit was caused by their father, but remember that everyone has inherited this spirit from their original parents, Adam and Eve. The prodigal son wants nothing to do with his loving father and so demands his inheritance and goes out and squanders it. Before Christ we are all like him. We want our independence—we want to do it our way, and we don't want God's interference.

We can become self-centered, self-reliant, controlling, manipulative, and the list goes on and on. Eventually, the prodigal comes to his senses, returns home and for the first time realizes who his father truly is and who he is in him—a beloved son.

The elder son is the perfect example of one who has been captured by an orphan spirit. He looks on his brother and the celebration of his return with disdain. After all, his younger brother had treated his father with great disrespect, while he had been doing all that was required of him, performing to perfection! But the truth is that he hadn't done so out of love for his father; he had labored on a daily basis to receive his father's approval and validation, toiling as a slave instead of a beloved son.

The father's response, *"'Son, you are always with me, and all that I have is yours,'"* is an amazing revelation of the Father's heart to you and me: "Son, you are always with me—all of the resources of My kingdom are at your disposal." Yet many have shied away from an intimate relationship with the Father because they don't know Him. We have to ask ourselves, "Why?"

This was the point that Jesus was trying to get across to the Pharisees, but they just couldn't understand. They were bound by the traditions of time, operating under a religious spirit that said, "This is what you must do in order to be acceptable before the Lord."

The Father's response is still the same: *"Son,* daughter [author's addition], *you are always with me, and all that I have is yours."* The problem is that we don't fully believe it. We have allowed the enemy's lies to so penetrate our hearts that it has damaged our spiritual eyesight, preventing us from seeing and experiencing the Father.

Several years ago, I was involved in a mentoring relationship with two young people who were much like this second son. Both had graduated from one of the most prestigious law schools in America. Both loved the Lord, were actively involved in ministry, and were highly successful in their fields of work. As I got to know them, I discovered that they were both driven by perfectionism, a true sign of an orphan spirit. Both had incredible work ethics, but it seemed the harder they worked and served, the higher the performance bar would move. It was one that could never be mastered but it was mastering them. This proved true not only in their secular work but also in their relationship with the Lord.

A Slave or a Beloved Son or Daughter

A slave leads someone to a master; a beloved son or daughter leads them to a father.

The second, seemingly obedient son in the parable of the *Prodigal Son* was totally unaware of who he was. He was a beloved son—not for what he did, but *for who he was.* Today the church is filled with believers who view God through the same distorted lens that the second son used. The enemy uses the same lie today that He spoke to Eve in the garden, *"You will not surely die… your eyes will be opened, and you will be like God knowing good and evil."* Contrary to what Satan promised, their vision became distorted, and they viewed God not as a loving Father but as one who was distant and unsafe. They viewed Him as one who required their performance in order to gain His approval, and this is what the older brother in the parable believed as well. Yet, he was in the father's house and all that the father had was his, not because of his performance, but because he truly was the father's beloved son.

Many Christians respond to God much like this young man responded to his father. But it is just as Paul wrote in his letter to the believers in Galatia who had begun to return to the works of the law:

> *For by grace you have been saved through faith, and that not of yourselves; it is the gift of God, not of works, lest anyone should boast. (Eph. 2:8-9)*

CHAPTER 5

CAPTIVES

---

*God is not the director of an orphanage; He is
a Father looking for someone who will dream.*[9]

The Bondage of a Religious Spirit

The orphan spirit attempts to rise up in each of us for the sole purpose of skewing our vision of whom our Father is and whom we are in Him. If we allow it, the orphan spirit will intimidate us into performing—keeping the law instead of resting and abiding in the finished work of Christ. Agreeing with this orphan spirit leads us into the bondage of a religious spirit.

One woman, Jenny, was taught that when bad things happen to you, it is because *you* are bad and so God has to balance things out and punish you. Her parents told her that she was God's punishment to them, and when Jenny found herself in Stage IV cancer, she viewed it from that perspective. She told her friends that she wasn't afraid of dying, but she was afraid of the disgust that she would see on God's face when they met.

Is it really true that some see Him this way? What kind of Father is that? We need to clarify that God the Father is not different in nature and character from His Son. As we look at God's Word, we can learn to know the Father by looking at His Son. Reading about the life of Christ, observing His interactions with individuals, and studying the stories and parables that He shared, we will be able to observe the true nature of our Heavenly Father.

> *"…no one knows the Son except the Father. Nor does anyone know the Father except the Son, and the one to whom the Son wills to reveal Him." (Matt. 11:27)*

We can't trust Him if we don't know in the very core of our being that God exists and that He loves us. Without trusting Him, we can never know who we truly are. The wonderful truth is that God already knows who you really are and that is whom He loves!

Compassion and Mercy

This merciful heart of God is revealed as Jesus was hanging on the cross with two criminals being crucified on either side of Him.

> *Then one of the criminals who were hanged blasphemed Him, saying, "If You are the Christ, save Yourself and us."*
>
> *But the other, answering, rebuked him, saying, "Do you not even fear God, seeing you are under the same condemnation? And we indeed justly, for we receive the due reward of our deeds; but this Man has done nothing wrong." Then he said to Jesus, "Lord, remember me when You come into Your kingdom."*
>
> *And Jesus said to him, "Assuredly, I say to you, today you will be with Me in Paradise." (Luke 23:39-43)*

What does this reveal to you of the heart of God? These men are criminals, receiving deserved punishment for crimes they had committed. One just wants out of the situation he finds himself in. The other one recognizes who he is and sees it as the inevitable consequence of his crime; his words are spoken from a humble, repentant heart.

Surely these men had heard the lies of the enemy about who they were and about their destiny and purpose in life. It's possible that they had been abandoned by their own fathers. Here, they find themselves in incredible pain, suffering torment for their crimes—one filled with rage; the other with a repentant heart. God cared for both of them equally; yet only one would see and cry out, *"Lord, remember me when You come into Your kingdom."* The man was pleading, "Please don't abandon me!"

From all eternity the Father knew this man, and through the suffering of His Son,

He revealed His heart of compassion and mercy to him, *"Assuredly, I say to you, today you will be with Me in Paradise.*

Prior to visiting a prison for women, William Paul Young, author of *The Shack*, sent his book to each one of the inmates. After sharing with the women, one came up to him with tears in her eyes and asked him, "Do you think that the Father is fond of me?"

We see God's love and compassion revealed when Young replied, "He is *especially* fond of you."

We Are the Ones He Left the Ninety-Nine to Find!

Then all the tax collectors and the sinners drew near to Him to hear Him. And the Pharisees and scribes complained, saying, "This Man receives sinners and eats with them."

So He spoke this parable to them, saying: "What man of you, having a hundred sheep, if he loses one of them, does not leave the ninety-nine in the wilderness, and go after the one which is lost until he finds it? And when he has found it, he lays it on his shoulders, rejoicing. And when he comes home, he calls together his friends and neighbors, saying to them, 'Rejoice with me, for I have found my sheep which was lost!' I say to you that likewise there will be more joy in heaven over one sinner who repents than over ninety-nine just persons who need no repentance. (Luke 15:1-7)

In Jesus' day, the tax collectors were hated above all people. They worked for the Roman government in order to extract taxes that cut deeply into the people's livelihood. However, through this story, Jesus revealed the heart of the Father for them. Like all of us, they were broken, lost, and without hope. Yet, these are the ones Jesus came to save, deliver, and set free.

God loves us even in our brokenness and failures, pursuing us in His great love. He does this in order to heal us and restore our true identity.

It is a process, and process is what relationship is all about. The most fundamental truth about the nature and character of God is that He is a relational being. Father, Son, and Holy Spirit have been in relationship forever.[10]

If we allow Him, God will come and heal us from the inside out! The fundamental problem is that many believers, having been captured by an orphan spirit, struggle with the reality that God is good. Because of wounds they have received, this spirit has progressively taken over their hearts to the point where their spiritual vision has become severely distorted. Even when they read of the love of God, they find it hard to embrace His love personally. As they look into the mirror, they continue to agree with the lies that the enemy has spoken over them, much like the woman who was dying of cancer who believed that it was a result of God punishing her. What an incredible lie about the goodness and kindness of the Father.

I remember the time when I struggled with the idea that someday I would stand before the Judgment Seat of God. I had such horrible fear. What would it be like? How would He judge me? What did I need to do to satisfy Him in order that He wouldn't be disappointed with me, like my earthly father was? As I struggled with this thought, the Lord began to speak to me. "Son, when that time comes I will not only be in front of you, but beside you and in you; you have nothing to fear." Such love overwhelmed me in that moment—I felt so free!

In the last hours before Jesus went to the cross, He promised that He would send the Holy Spirit, saying, *"I will not leave you orphans" (John 14:18)*.

Jesus sensed that His disciples were feeling like orphans. Where did this feeling come from? It came from the beginning of time and has continued down through time as the enemy comes to all of mankind declaring that God has deserted His people. This very feeling was overwhelming the disciples, but Jesus assured them that although He would leave them, He would not leave them alone; He would send His Holy Spirit. Jesus dealt with this orphan spirit for the last time at the Cross, and from that point on, we as believers have had the ability to overcome it.

On the cross, one of the last statements that Jesus made was, *"My God, My God, why have You forsaken Me?" (Matt. 27:46)*. All of our sins, diseases, and afflictions were placed upon Jesus on the cross and the judgment of God was released in full measure upon His Son in order to satisfy the justice of God. God took sin upon Himself through the physical body of Jesus and accomplished what the law never could.

One of those afflictions was an orphan spirit that has passed down through the spiritual DNA of mankind to you and me. But on the cross of Jesus an incredible exchange occurred—Jesus took the orphan spirit, giving us the opportunity to exchange it for sonship. For all who by faith believe in Jesus the Son of God, this exchange becomes available the moment you repent of your sins and give your heart to Jesus. Now we are no longer orphans but beloved sons and beloved daughters. Our agreement with God empowers His truth in our lives and sets us free.

> *You are all sons of God through faith in Christ Jesus. (Gal. 3:26)*

> *And because you are sons, God has sent forth the Spirit of His Son into your hearts, crying out, "Abba, Father!" Therefore you are no longer a slave but a son, and if a son, then an heir of God through Christ. (Gal. 4:6-7)*

You and I have a clear assignment and that is to "exhibit the multifaceted wisdom of God" on the earth now. As we do, we "release…His purpose in and through us to the world around us." To do so is to walk in the fullness of Genesis 1:28 as "His delegated authority on this planet."

"A reformation has begun. And at the heart of this great move of the Spirit is the total TRANSFORMATION of the people of God as they discover their true identity and purpose."[9]

Each of us, as beloved sons and daughters, has been born for the purpose of walking in partnership with our Heavenly Father, bringing the evidence and fruit of the kingdom of God into the areas that we influence. As His sons and daughters, we must be gripped with the urgency to know the Father's heart in order to clearly hear what the Spirit of God is saying. We must allow God to free us from the lies and wounds in our lives that have caused our eyesight to become twisted from the truth of whom the Father is and whom we become by entering into Him.

> *For the earnest expectation of the creation eagerly waits for the revealing of the sons of God. (Rom. 8:19)*

As we walk with the Father in relationship, He can remove those things that have wrongly captured our hearts and heal wounds that have been inflicted upon us, restoring our true identity and the purpose for which we were created.

Only God is able to "unwind" the damage done in your life, without breaking or damaging you. [10]

All things have been delivered to Me by My Father, and no one knows the Son except the Father. Nor does anyone know the Father except the Son, and the one to whom the Son wills to reveal Him. (Matt. 11:27)

God Desires to Heal Us

The Father's invitation is for us to experience Him now. That was Jesus' request to the Father as He prayed *"and this is eternal life that they might know You" (John 17:3)*. His invitation is for all who will come.

By choosing to continue on this journey, you have embarked on a lifetime adventure that is challenging, fun, and life-giving. You will receive the freedom found only in Christ from every wound and lie that has ever been spoken over you. For many of us, those lies have become the filter through which we process all of our thoughts about God, ourselves, and others.

About 700 years before Jesus was born, the prophet Isaiah wrote these words:

"Behold! My Servant whom I uphold, My Elect One in whom My soul delights! I have put My Spirit upon Him; He will bring forth justice to the Gentiles. He will not cry out, nor raise His voice, Nor cause His voice to be heard in the street. A bruised reed He will not break, And smoking flax He will not quench; He will bring forth justice for truth. (Is. 42:1-3)

"The Spirit of the Lord God is upon Me, Because the Lord has anointed Me To preach good tidings to the poor; He has sent Me to heal the brokenhearted, To proclaim liberty to the captives, And the opening of the prison to those who are bound; To proclaim the acceptable year of the Lord, And the day of vengeance of our God; To comfort all who mourn, To console those who mourn in Zion, To give them beauty for ashes, The oil of joy for mourning, The garment of praise for the spirit of heaviness; That they may be called trees of righteousness, The planting of the Lord, that He may be glorified." And they shall rebuild the old ruins, They shall raise up the former desolations, And they shall repair the ruined cities, The desolations of many generations. (Is. 61:1-4)

These prophetic revelations of the Messiah reveal the mission of Christ and the heart of the Father. To all who put their trust and hope in the finished work of the Cross, each attribute depicted becomes a living promise, providing the healing and freedom that each of us needs.

Captured Hearts

Most of us came into the kingdom of God through faith in Christ but still broken and captive in one way or another. We need to be free and we want to be free. But before that can happen, we must allow the Holy Spirit to reveal those things that have captured our hearts.

Recently, I read about a man who at the age of four watched the police lead his father away in handcuffs; he never saw him again. He was raised by a godly mother, but their lives were filled with incredible poverty. In the midst of this hopeless situation, however, God spoke lovingly to him, calling him His son.

His heart yearned for a father who would spend time with him, enjoying conversations that only a father and son could have. Longingly, he would sit on his front porch as the cars passed by his home "imagining that one day one would park and the man getting out would be my daddy—but it never happened." His father died when he was only 18. He said he remembered peering into the casket at the face of his father and never shedding a tear. "Killed in a car accident, he died drunk, leaving me hobbled by the sorrow of years of fatherlessness."

Years later, he would come to his father's gravesite and begin to tell his father about the man he had become and how he wished his father had been in his life. The same question he asked himself that day is one that many of us have asked, "Why didn't he want me, why didn't he take the time to know me?"

Fatherlessness and abandonment in the heart of a child create tremendous wounding. Children like this spend the rest of their days attempting to win the approval of men and women, searching for the love and validation they never received from their earthly father. This abandonment, with its lack of validation, has defined for many of us who we *think* we should be, but it is not what God created us to be.

Vows

Vows have a huge impact on our relationship with our Heavenly Father. A very good friend of mine, Nathan Daniel, author of *Freedom Through Forgiveness*, shared with me about the negative impact vows can have on our lives. He shared from his counseling experience about a woman who had made a vow as a result of being deeply wounded by someone. She had vowed that she would never allow *anyone* to get close to her again for fear of being hurt.

Years later this vow impacted both her marriage and her relationship with God. As she told him her story, she told him she couldn't understand why she struggled so much in her relationship with God.

My friend explained to her, "When you said *anyone*, that included God."

Her vow had kept her from allowing God into her heart, preventing an intimate relationship with Him. Once this was revealed to her, she repented, breaking her agreement with the vow she had made years ago. Her heart that had been held captive by this vow was then opened up to the love of the Father and her husband.

Many of us have made vows just like this woman; however, as you can see, when we make vows that are in response to hurt, pain, and wounding, we give the enemy a portal by which he can enter and take over our hearts. As it says in Isaiah 61, Jesus came to set the captive free and to open the prison door. We must break agreement with the vow or vows we have made, nail them to the Cross of Christ, forgive the one who may have hurt us, and then we can ask the Father what He has for us in place of the vow.

When we are wounded or lied to, our defense mechanisms rise up, and we can make vows that will capture our hearts and our destinies forever. Prayerfully consider if you have made any vows that have impacted your heart and your relationship with the Father. If you have, let the Holy Spirit reveal them to you so that you can be set free and walk in this great liberty that Paul writes of in Galatians:

> *Stand fast therefore in the liberty by which Christ has made us free, and do not be entangled again with a yoke of bondage. (Gal. 5:1)*

For some, the abandonment is a literal physical separation, but in my case and the case of many others, the man who was called my father was physically present but absent in so many other ways The very man that God created to be my example and role model was one from whom I had no interest in learning anything. His lack of fathering brought me such pain that I vowed early in life that I would never be anything like my father. That vow led to a snare.

Before my grandfather died, I had been innocent and relatively carefree; my grandfather had in many ways filled in where my own father had neglected to father me. But when he died, all that was lost and I felt so alone. As I shared earlier, I remember being constantly compared to my sister. She was an incredible student and excelled in everything she did. Why couldn't I be like her? This constant comparison led me to believe that I was a loser. Comparing ourselves to others hinders our unique identity, created by God for His pleasure and for our greatest good.

My father wasn't there when I needed him the most. He was never able to see the gifts and callings in my life or to call out my destiny, and his constant criticism of me encouraged the lie that I was a failure. Agreeing with this lie, my heart became locked up, preventing me from becoming the unique person God had made me to be. Feeling insecure and unsafe, fear of man and fear of failure dominated me and became a familiar theme in my life. Then with my grandfather's death, I felt completely abandoned.

To be fair, my father had faced his own share of trauma in life. The example his own father set for him was very domineering, controlling, and filled with anger. My father was just 24 years old when his father committed suicide. I can't imagine what that must have done to him.

It was many years before my father met Jesus and his life began to change; later in life, he lived in great regret. Although he was saved, I know my dad feared standing before Jesus. His fear was unfounded because when Jesus died for him, His blood had cleansed him from all unrighteousness. But he just couldn't get beyond the past. The enemy would torment and lie to him, and he would agree. I don't think my father knew his Heavenly Father in the way that the Lord desired. He does now, but God doesn't want us to wait until we die and go to heaven to have this relationship. He wants us to have the same face-to-face relationship with Him as Jesus does, and it is possible for all of us right now.

I longed for relationship with my earthly father. I yearned for his approval, validation, and for his love; yet, it wasn't to be. But then my Heavenly Father came at just the right time, touching the deep need in my heart that He, and He alone, could meet.

When we open our hearts to the spirit of abandonment, it will cause us to see ourselves through the lens of our relationship with our earthly fathers. This is how orphans view God. Abandonment, wounds, and lies by an earthly father will pervert our perception of God, causing us to project our relationship with our earthly father onto God.

A spirit of abandonment brings rejection with it. It results in performance and in procrastination, but more than that, it results in a desire to be accepted. Instead of living our lives as beloved sons and daughters, we live them as slaves, performing for a master with the hope of getting His approval and validation.

God is the initiator. He initiated the creation of mankind. He initiated relationship with man in the Garden, and as a loving, non-condemning Father, continues to initiate relationships with you and me that will last through all eternity.

CHAPTER 6

IN SEARCH OF A FATHER'S BLESSING

୬୬୬୬

Tom's Testimony

(The name has been changed to protect his privacy.

I remember as a young boy that something was missing in my life. I had no idea what until I was approaching the end of high school and going to college. Then I realized I needed to grow up and hear from a spiritual father.

When I was eleven or twelve years old, I remember feeling a disconnection from my dad. He had played with me and usually had time to throw the baseball with me. He coached me in baseball when I was ten or so, and I remember baseball being something I loved. I was not an easy preteen, and I take responsibility for my lack of respect and not listening to my dad.

My father had always worked nights as long as I could remember. He was a super hard worker and definitely passed this character trait down to me. I tried to give the best effort I could to whatever I was doing in order to gain approval. My dad hardly ever came to my games because of his work schedule, but I thought he could have come to more games to support me in what I loved. I felt that I wasn't valued by him and felt rejected.

Around this time, I remember praying to receive Jesus into my heart. I do not have a lot of childhood memories, but I do remember that specific night making the decision to follow Jesus. As a result, some major changes took place in my life. I remember loving to read God's Word, taking notes, and memorizing lots of Scripture. I had a really bad mouth and used to curse all the time before I met Jesus, but I immediately stopped cursing and began to hang out with really different friends.

This is when I turned to basketball as my number one sport and played in my first games as an eighth grader. I played a lot of basketball but was not really skilled and relied on hard work and athleticism to make an impact. I remember very clearly wanting to do things my way and not being open to coaching due to not wanting to be controlled. It is funny to me now because I put a huge premium on being coachable and being a great teammate. I really learned what not to be as a player throughout my career. I thought I was a team player at the time but really never bought in fully. I got better each year, but looking back, I see ways I could have been a better teammate and player.

When I finished high school, I felt lost. I set off to play basketball and go to Bible college but only lasted one semester. It was then the Lord began to work in my life; I was willing to be fathered. A man that became my spiritual father had spent some time with me and challenged me in my walk with the Lord. Only a few people had ever done that in my life, but this man was not a pastor, a teacher, or a coach of mine. He really had no reason to spend time, effort, and energy on me.

This is when I began to realize the true Father heart of God—He came, accepting me with no strings attached. I had always felt like when I was doing well the Father accepted me, but when I was struggling, I would fall away from Him and think I was not a beloved son. This man, Mr. Jim, has taught me the love of the Father. He always has time for me, encourages me, prays for me, and loves me—no matter what. Although he has two of his own sons, I really feel like I am also his son.

I think much of my coaching career has been trying to prove I could be great at something. This is a typical response to a need to be fathered. I wanted so much to be unconditionally loved and validated in what I did. Each time I accomplished something as a coach, I always hoped my dad would take the initiative to tell me he was proud of me for spending my life trying to make a difference in young men's lives.

There are many days I experience doubt. I doubt the Lord's involvement in my life even though it is unmistakable that He is not only involved but doing His work. I doubt who I am in Christ, my abilities, and even my ability to be a husband and father. I doubt my ability as a coach and always think I could have done better. I am always thinking, "Is there a way that I can do something that will make my earthly father take notice?" Why do I think I need my father to acknowledge me?

This year marks the seventeenth year in which I have invested in the lives of young men. I have coached basketball with high school student athletes and have been successful both on and off the court—off the court, seeing young men accept Christ, be changed, and begin to be focused on others. On the court, I've had 214 wins and 79 losses in 10 seasons as the head boys' basketball coach. In 293 games—73% of the games I have coached in—I have been blessed to win as well as our final fours, and I have coached in two state championship games which we won in 2012 and 2013. In 2012 we were 27-4 and ranked in the top ten in the country in three different high school basketball polls.

I really thought this kind of success would bring my father around to somehow show me I am accepted. I'm not sure what I was looking for from my father but it is still the same. There is a father-shaped void in my heart. I really just desire my father's acknowledgement, I think. I can't fully explain it, but I guess I feel orphaned. Who am I? Who is my father?

I've known this young man for over 18 years. He is a wonderful husband, father, coach, and mentor. His life testimony is not at all uncommon, though. The greatest desire that each of us has is for an earthly father who accepts and loves us where we are in life, acknowledging who we are and who we will become. As of this writing, Tom has yet to receive these things from his father and his heart cries out, "Why? Why didn't he want me? What is wrong with me?" At times like this, the enemy comes and lies to us, attempting to veil the truth of who our Heavenly Father is and how He sees us.

Tom said at the end of his testimony that although he is not sure what he was looking for from his father, nothing has changed his father's heart or their relationship. In his desire for validation and acknowledgment from his father, Tom strove to perform to meet the highest standards, but that didn't fill the "father-shaped void" in his heart. He still feels orphaned and is struggling for identity after all of these years. Though he still wrestles with the question of why his earthly father won't acknowledge him, at least Tom knows today who he is before the Father.

When we feel abandoned by the one who should love us and lead us, the enemy uses the lie that there is something wrong with us. We agree with this lie, and then set out to do whatever is necessary in order to gain our father's love and respect.

Many in the body of Christ have been raised in this type of fatherless environment, and when they come into the kingdom, they continue to perform in order to get the Father's attention and approval. Instead of seeing themselves as beloved sons and daughters, they remain slaves driven to achieve in order to get the Father's pleasure. It is an orphan spirit—an identity that has been formed and fashioned by wounds and lies. They find it more comfortable to live under the law than to live a life that reflects the freedom that Christ has called them into. God wants to replace that false identity with our true identity.

Many stay in this place, fearing that if they don't do all the right things, then their salvation will be in jeopardy. This attitude reflects their personal view of who the Father is and who they are in Him.

Our Heavenly Father is the One that began a good work in our lives, giving us the gift of faith so that we could respond to the invitation of Christ. The Apostle Paul refers to this in his letter to the Philippians:

> *Being confident of this, that He who began a good work in you will carry it on to completion until the day of Jesus Christ. (Philippians 1:6)*

The enemy wants us to think that this is too easy. He wants us to think that everything we have ever gotten we had to get on our own, and we fear that if we don't do something, we won't receive the reward He has for us. It is a lie. To embrace the truth is to embrace His love which casts out all fear. Fear causes torment, but love brings peace and joy.

When you and I embrace the truth, then our hearts can respond to our loving Father who cares about the smallest of details in our lives. Then we can walk in obedience not out of obligation but out of our love for Him. God's work at the cross stands as the undeniable proof that we are loved and are beloved sons and daughters of God.

Fear of abandonment isn't new, having begun back in the Garden of Eden. It was one of the last things that Jesus addressed as He spoke His final words to His disciples before going to the cross to bear this wicked iniquity in His own body as He died on the cross.

In the last few hours before going to the cross, Jesus began to address the fears that each of the disciples had in their hearts. They had heard Him say a number of times that He would suffer many things and die. How could this be? They thought that He was the conquering Messiah and that He would restore the kingdom of Israel. Now, hours before His death, He once again spoke of His departure.

What must they have felt? I believe the fear of abandonment began to creep its way into their thoughts. Jesus began to speak words of comfort to them.

"And I will pray the Father, and He will give you another Helper, that He may abide with you forever— the Spirit of truth, whom the world cannot receive, because it neither sees Him nor knows Him; but you know Him, for He dwells with you and will be in you. I will not leave you orphans; I will come to you." (John 14:18)

"Peace I leave with you, My peace I give to you, not as the world gives do I give to you. Let not your heart be troubled, neither let it be afraid." (John 14:27)

Why would He say this? He knew it was the same feeling that Adam and Eve had in the garden, and it is the same feeling that many of us have experienced in one measure or another in our lifetime. We inherited this orphan spirit from our original parents, but now Jesus has come to break its stronghold over our lives, setting free anyone who will receive Him (See Isaiah 61:1-3). This spirit can only have influence in our lives if we allow it!

And about the ninth hour Jesus cried out with a loud voice, saying, "Eli, Eli lama sabachthani?" that is, "My God, My God, why have You forsaken Me?" (Matt. 27:46)

According to Isaiah 53, Jesus bore all of the brokenness and sin of mankind from the time man was created until the end of this age when He died on the cross. This included the lie that God had abandoned them when He placed Adam and Eve outside the Garden. This orphan spirit was dealt with, once and for all, that dark afternoon two thousand years ago. God's justice was fully satisfied and His infinite love was fully expressed through the finished work of the Cross.

The work the Father and Son accomplished together…to destroy its power and offer a way for humanity to be rescued from the brokenness of sin, to recapture the relationship God had always wanted with His people." "God was fully involved in all aspects of this incredible plan…It's important that we see them working together, enduring the process necessary to destroy sin and liberating those they loved. Jesus was not the victim and the Father the victimizer. They were executing a plan they, the Father, Son and Holy Spirit had devised on the day they first decided to create a man and woman. They would pay the price together for the relationship they so deeply desired to share with us. [11]

For He made Him who knew no sin to be sin for us, that we might become the righteousness of God in Him. (2 Cor. 5:21)

Why then do so many struggle with their true identity as beloved sons and daughters of God?

The Effects of Childhood

The answer to living a fruitful Christian life is waking up each day in the knowledge that you are already beloved. The day I woke up and heard the Lord say to me,

"I am so content with you," I not only felt validated but I felt loved and desired. I had never experienced anything like that from my earthly father. Words such as these set our hearts free and transform us into all that He created us to be.

Without a healthy view in our hearts of how the Father sees us, even in our immaturity, we will not be able to experience intimacy with the Father as His beloved son or daughter.

The following is a story of a dear friend whose life was so impacted by words that wounded the very core of his being that he set out on a journey in order to prove himself and to attempt to discover his purpose in life.

Wounds Caused by Words: A Defining Moment

ॐॐॐॐ

Brian's Testimony:
(The name has been changed to protect his privacy.)

A good friend of mine, Brian, was a senior-level executive for several corporations that were listed as the top 50 by *Fortune Magazine*. He had all the wealth that a man could dream of having. Yet, even with all that, he really wasn't who God had designed him to be. He was driven by a vow that he had made at the age of thirteen in response to a comment by his father. That one comment became what he called "a defining moment."

His father owned an air conditioning and heating company. Brian was daydreaming while working alongside his father one day, when his father suddenly interrupted his reverie saying, "You had better get a good education, because you are not going to make a living with your hands." What he really heard his father saying was "You don't have what it takes to make it in 'my' world."

Hurt and filled with shame, he began to believe the lie that he didn't belong. His heart's desire was to work alongside his father, "but I knew I didn't meet his expectations."

Brian made a vow that day, "I will be more successful than any of the men that I know…. I am going to do whatever it takes to be rich and I will create my own circle of friends."

Brian's heart became driven with a lust for power, influence, and wealth. As he rose in position in the corporate world, he was nicknamed "Iceman" by coworkers. Those wounds from his youth drove him on a quest to find acceptance, love, and validation.

He became a perfectionist, which impacted not only those who worked with him but those closest to him—his family.

Brian's perspective of God became distorted, and as a result, impacted not only the way he viewed himself but how he responded to life and others and how he viewed the Father God. Brian is on the same journey as each of us, growing in his relationship with the Father—discovering more each day of who the Father is and who he is in Him.

☙☙☜☜

At least in some measure, I believe many of us have experienced the same thing Brian has and we also struggle with our perception of the Father. The Father's character has been marred and misinterpreted through the lens of our own pain. Many of us have had similar experiences with our earthly fathers that have caused us to put up a protective shield of a false self. Yet that protective shield becomes one of the greatest deterrents to our developing a loving relationship with our Heavenly Father.

Brian's journey can define many of us who have been wounded by demeaning words spoken over our lives.

The void left in our hearts by our unfulfilled desire to be unconditionally loved sends us on a journey to achieve validation and approval, with the hope that our earthly fathers will grant us the same. Many of us have poured our lives into whatever we do to succeed at whatever cost; we find our value and significance in success. Yet, at best, it is a false attempt driven by the pain of rejection.

Like with Brian, many words that are spoken over us or to us in our youth leave lasting impressions in our lives. Children are so vulnerable and the enemy uses that for an opportunity to break into their lives with the orphan spirit.

In the same way, words or acts of kindness can *also* have a lasting impression on us.

Over the years, I have encountered individuals who showed kindness or goodness to me. One such person was an African-American lady my parents employed to do our housework and to care for us when I was a child. There were times when she would babysit for us while my parents went out for the evening. Her kindness made an incredible impression upon me as a young child, and although she was materially very poor, I look upon her today as one of the richest people I have ever known. I look forward to the day when I will see her in heaven. I am convinced that I am writing this today because of her kindness, tenderness, and love that I needed so desperately as a child.

> "…not knowing that the goodness of God leads you to repentance." (Rom. 2:4)

The kindness of people can do good things in our lives, but God's kindness is far greater; it leads us to repentance and brings us into reconciliation where we can enjoy a relationship with our Heavenly Father.

Healing Comes Through a Revelation of the Father

My son, give me your heart, And let your eyes observe my ways. (Prov. 23:26)

As we observe the life of Christ, we will discover the heart and the ways of the Father. As we observe Jesus' interaction with those He created, we will discover that, amazingly, the redemptive plan of God was not just for the salvation of the soul of man but also for the spiritual, physical, and emotional healing of mankind. Through Christ's life we see the accurate revelation of the heart of the Father.

God's incredible gift of salvation brings with it freedom. Through God's marvelous gift of His Son and the Cross, we have been liberated from the tyranny of sin, the lies of the enemy, and the wounds and pains inflicted upon our lives. And we have been brought into an incredible freedom whereby we can walk in liberty as the sons of God.

We are the only ones that can keep ourselves from this freedom. So as we continue our journey, remain open to the Holy Spirit. Ask Him what things He wants to show you that have hindered your walk with the Father. Be willing to surrender to Him and be confident that He has your best interests in mind. Even more than you do, He desires for you to be all that God has destined for you to be—not only in this life but in eternity.

CHAPTER 7

THE FATHER IS FURTHER REVEALED

As we read about Jesus interacting with broken humanity, it becomes very obvious that He did indeed come to declare the Good News of the Gospel. We see Him healing the brokenhearted, setting the captives free, opening the prison doors to those who are bound, proclaiming the acceptable year of the Lord, and comforting all who mourn as was prophesied in Isaiah 61:1-2. Jesus always reflected the heart of our Father in all that He did on the earth.

My Introduction to the Father

Maria's Testimony
(The name has been changed to protect her privacy.

It was my birthday weekend. Little did I know, the morning of my birthday, the Lord would give me a picture that changed my whole thought process about Him. As I stood worshiping, I saw myself sitting on my Father's lap. It surprised me a bit because I have never really had this picture before. As I sat there, my right cheek resting on His chest, I placed my very small hand in His very large one. I did not hold His hand. I just let my hand rest in the palm of His. I remember that I could see His robe which was very white. I could see His upturned hand. I could also see His hair and beard which were both so white and so very soft. I could not see His face. That did not disturb me as much as I thought it would. Rather, it created a deep longing. I believe He will show me more of Himself in His timing.

This picture stayed with me all through the weekend. At one point, I sat there and asked my Father, "Am I a bad girl?" I knew that it sounded so childish and I was a little embarrassed to ask it. But I knew this is how I felt so much of the time. I could never do anything right. I always felt the heavy pressure of failure weighing on me.

He answered me with such clarity. In fact, I am not sure I have ever heard His voice so clearly before. He said to me, "You NEVER disappoint Me. You NEVER disappoint Me." He repeated this over and over again. The word "never" was so loud, resounding as if reaching a thousand hallways. Scenes of my past failures kept popping up in my head and He answered each one by saying, "You NEVER disappoint Me." All of a sudden, my view of the Father changed from stern, disappointed God sitting on His distant throne, to my Daddy, One who had truly never left me; One who had never held unreasonable expectations of me. I had spoken of His love all of my Christian life, but it had never been a reality until that moment. I finally met my Abba.

All through the weekend, I experienced His kindness. I felt it pour over me like oil. He is so affectionate, so ready to share His joy. I felt His delight, His pleasure in me. "How can this be?" I asked over and over again.

"I delight in you," He responded each time. Abba's love actually feels different from His Son's. I have experienced the intense love of the Son. I have gained a little understanding of the passionate pursuit of my Bridegroom. But this felt so different, so kind and so very tender; soft, yet with an undercurrent of power that knows no depth. I can now call myself "daughter" and truly mean it.

The evening of my birthday, I had an amazing experience. It was my formal introduction to the Father. As I sat there, I saw Jesus. It was such a moment of recognition for me. "Oh, I know You," my heart cried out.

He walked toward me and took me by the hand. He led me to the Father, who was standing there waiting. Jesus turned to me and said, "I want you to meet my Father." Then He said something that set me free for eternity. "And I don't want you to be afraid of Him." I knew He did not mean for me to lay down my holy fear that naturally comes with walking in relationship with the Lord, but I had unholy fear of my Abba. It was fear that prevented me from running to Him when I made mistakes. I had made it a habit to run far, far away from Him almost every time. I still have much to learn in this area but I now know I have a very patient, kind Father who will teach me.

Our Father Is Safe—He Is the Shepherd

One of the first things you will discover about our Father is that He is safe. Every word Jesus spoke and everything He did reflected the heart of the Father, and multitudes followed after Him. Having lived under the tyranny of the legalistic leaders of the day, the hearts of these people were desperate. They carried the wounds of the religious spirits of the age, and their lives were a spiritual desert. Sheep without a shepherd, they craved love and acceptance, and they longed to be cared for. When Jesus came, His actions and words revealed Him as the Good Shepherd. He was a safe haven and they were drawn to Him.

Several years ago, I read about a tour group in Israel. As they traveled through the countryside, one of the tourists saw a man driving a flock of sheep. He said to the tour guide, "That must be the shepherd."

"No," the tour guide replied, "he is the butcher. A shepherd doesn't drive the sheep, he leads them." That sounds just like the Shepherd in Psalm 23, doesn't it? That is who Jesus is!

> *The Lord is my shepherd; I shall not want. He makes me to lie down in green pastures; He leads me beside the still waters. He restores my soul; He leads me in the paths of righteousness for His name's sake. (Ps. 23:1-3)*

As the Good Shepherd, His words and the miracles He performed demonstrated the Father's heart.

> *"I am the good shepherd. The good shepherd gives His life for the sheep." (John 10:11)*

Laboring Under the Misconceptions of Religious Spirits

Many have tremendous misconceptions of our Heavenly Father. For many, the lies and wounds of life have become the web by which the enemy spins his wicked lies to cloud our perception of who our Heavenly Father truly is. He uses his lies to make us afraid of the One who loves us unconditionally. This fear causes us to feel unsafe in His presence and to run *away from* Him instead of *toward* Him.

Through these deceptions, mankind has developed a belief that God would never want us in our brokenness—but the truth is He does. He calls out to us through His Word, demonstrating His objective of restoring mankind's relationship with the Father through every one of His personal encounters and every story and parable. Keep in mind that everything that Jesus did or spoke came directly from the Father. He did nothing on His own. We need to stop running away from Him, and let the Father draw us toward Him.

The religious leaders in Jesus' day used man-made laws for the purpose of keeping the people under their power and control. They were like the butcher herding the sheep rather than the shepherd leading them. They provided the dos and don'ts—if you do these things, God will be pleased with you; if you don't, then God will be displeased. As the people labored under these heavy burdens, the enemy was able to snatch away the joy of knowing God and having a relationship with their Creator.

Just as at the time of Christ, many people in churches today have been snared by a religious spirit that demands works in order to please God. In many Christian communities, the people function as slaves instead of beloved sons and daughters. They are orphans, driven to perform in order to get the attention and approval of their Father.

As Jesus walked the land of Israel, He saw His beloved creation laboring under the heavy burdens of religious laws created by man. You can almost hear them as they gather around the dinner table saying, "It is impossible to fulfill all of these laws! The more I try, the more I fail. I am so weary of the struggle. How will I ever be able to measure up to what God wants out of me? He can't possibly love me."

Imagine Jesus coming into this lovely town by the Sea of Galilee and seeing the lives of those whom He created in His image bearing the burdens of these man-made laws. He knew how the religious spirits had captured their hearts; and He issued an invitation of hope:

Come to Me, all you who are weary and burdened, and I will give you rest. Take My yoke upon you and learn from Me, for I am gentle and humble in heart, and you will find rest for your souls." (Matt. 11:28-29 NIV)

This invitation is still good for us today. Jesus comes with His message of hope, bringing rest for the weary and offering to take every weight and care off of our shoulders. I love this about Jesus!

The Servant Heart of God

Most of us have never considered servanthood as one of God's attributes. Yet we see it in the words of Isaiah the prophet: *"Behold! My Servant whom I uphold, My Elect One in whom My soul delights! I have put My Spirit upon Him…" (Is. 42:1)* We see this repeated by Jesus in Matthew 12:17-25 after He healed a man with a withered hand and then went on to heal a great multitude of people that followed after Him. This servanthood was expressed in the life of Jesus as He walked in absolute obedience to the Father. Reflecting only what He saw His Father doing and saying, servanthood was demonstrated by Jesus' actions. His life was our living example of the Word—the Word made flesh.

Jesus came as a servant, anointed with His Father's Spirit. He fully revealed this attribute of servanthood through His life; however, He never suspended any of His other attributes to fulfill this one.

"…just as the Son of Man did not come to be served, but to serve, and to give His life a ransom for many." (Matt. 20:28)

Through the years of His ministry Jesus served continuously, but there is one event that stands out to me more than any other.

And supper being ended, the devil having already put it into the heart of Judas Iscariot, Simon's son, to betray Him, Jesus, knowing that the Father had given all things into His hands, and that He had come from God and was going to God, rose from supper and laid aside His garments, took a towel and girded Himself. After that, He poured water into a basin and began to wash the disciples' feet, and to wipe them with the towel with which He was girded. (John 13:2-5)

And this was not the first time that God had knelt before His creation:

Then God blessed them, and God said to them, "Be fruitful and multiply; fill the earth and subdue it; have dominion over the fish of the sea, over the birds of the air, and over every living thing that moves on the earth." (Gen. 1:28)

The word *blessed* in the Hebrew means both "to bless" and "to kneel." As the Father began to declare both a blessing and a command over Adam and Eve, He knelt before them.

Again, we see the idea of God as a servant in Luke 12:

Blessed are those servants whom the master, when he comes, will find watching. Assuredly, I say to you that he will gird himself and have them sit down to eat, and will come and serve them. (Luke 12:37)

As we consider the prophetic word spoken in Isaiah 9, we see the idea of Him serving:

For unto us a Child is born, Unto us a Son is given; And the government will be upon His shoulder. And His name will be called Wonderful, Counselor, Mighty God, Everlasting Father, Prince of Peace. Of the increase of His government and peace there will be no end… (Is. 9:6-7)

Notice that the government of the kingdom of God *"will be upon His shoulders and it will increase, and His name will be called Wonderful, Counselor…"* Those who govern usually serve for the betterment of those they serve.

It is so incredible to imagine that the One who created you and me—the One who is our eternal Heavenly Father—is a servant. Be assured that I don't believe that God is a "genie in a bottle" that we can command at will. No, He is omnipotent, infinite, omniscient, omnipresent, King of Kings, and Lord of Lords, and He does not suspend any of His divine attributes as He communicates to you and me with a servant heart.

The lies of the enemy are destroyed as Jesus expresses His servant actions towards broken individuals. The veil that has blinded our eyes is removed so that we can see the truth of who the Father is.

Jesus is the sole expression of the Father, the perfect imprint of His nature.

Who being the brightness of His glory and the express image of His person, and upholding all things by the word of His power, when He had by Himself purged our sins, sat down at the right hand of the Majesty on high. (Heb. 1:3)

But at times we are like Philip was in John 14:7, wanting to know what our Heavenly Father is really like and not really understanding that we have already seen Him in Jesus.

Jesus' prayer to the Father in John 17 expresses the heart of God desiring that we come into an intimate relationship with Him:

And this is eternal life, that they may know You, the only true God, and Jesus Christ whom You have sent. (John 17:3)

Through each encounter Jesus had with others and the testimonies of individuals just like you and me, one or more of the attributes of God can be seen. His heart is revealed and we experience the prophetic words spoken of in Isaiah 61:1-3 and Isaiah 42:1-3, hundreds of years before Jesus was born. These same prophetic words are impacting the hearts and lives of individuals all over the world. Through these encounters we will begin to understand and know the Father and experience Him as never before. As you allow the Holy Spirit to reveal these truths to your hearts, He will set you free to be all that God has destined you to be.

Whether two thousand years ago or today, these encounters result in testimonies that bear witness to whom the Father really is. They reveal His infinite love and care for each one of us who have been made in His image. God wants to do in your life what He has done in the lives of so many throughout all of history.

Compassion

When people read stories about Jesus in the Bible, they tend to skim through them. It is important to take time to become engaged in the recorded accounts in the Gospel and to realize that these were real people facing circumstances that seemed impossible to them, but not to the Father. Let these stories come alive to you, imagining how these people must have felt. Observe the heart of the Father as it is expressed through the Son's words and actions. And see the prophecies from Isaiah 42 and 61 fully revealed through the life of Christ wherever He went.

Then Jesus went about all the cities and villages, teaching in their synagogues, preaching the gospel of the kingdom, and healing every sickness and every disease among the people. But when He saw the multitudes, He was moved with compassion for them, because they were weary and scattered, like sheep having no shepherd. (Matt. 9:35)

Compassion is defined as "a sympathetic consciousness of others' distress together with a desire to alleviate it." Reading through the Gospels, you find Jesus moved with compassion over and over again, expressing it for those who were like sheep without a shepherd, for those who were sick or diseased, and for the hungry. Moved by compassion, He would declare the Good News of the Gospel, bringing hope and healing.

The Miracle at Nain

Jesus healed a centurion's slave in Capernaum, and then traveled south to the city of Nain.

And when He came near the gate of the city, behold, a dead man was being carried out, the only son of his mother; and she was a widow. And a large crowd from the city was with her. When the Lord saw her, He had compassion on her and said to her, "Do not weep." Then He came and touched the open coffin, and those who carried him stood still. And He said, "Young man, I say to you, arise." So he who was dead sat up and began to speak. And He presented him to his mother. (Luke 7:12-15)

I can imagine Jesus approaching the crowd and encountering the widowed mother. He can feel the woman's grief, fear, hopelessness, and despair. I can hear His gentle voice filled with sorrow, *"Do not weep."* The Author of Life who would soon die for all pains, sorrow, grief, and sickness spoke with great compassion to this woman. His voice was the voice of the Father; His very nature was the Father's nature. Imagine what the woman must have felt, raising her tear-filled eyes to meet His; what she must have felt as her heart was instantly embraced by a love and a peace that was not from this world.

This woman may have seemed insignificant to many, but in the Father's eyes, she was His daughter. She was the daughter of a King. For Jesus to reach out and touch her son's coffin was totally out of character, never mind against their law, but that's just what Jesus did as He spoke to the corpse within saying, *"Young man, I say to you, arise."*

We see how the heart of Jesus was moved with compassion as He looked upon the mother. And we see the kindness of God as He cares for those things that impact peoples' lives. Where there is no hope, He is the God of hope. Where there is death and sorrow and pain in this life, He gives new life.

Life carries many joys, but at times it also brings great sadness. Yet, God is there with us—there is never a time He isn't present. Our Heavenly Father is not like any other person you or I have ever known. He has promised He will never leave us or forsake us. (See Hebrews 13:5.) He says that even though your mother or father forsakes you, He will not. (See Psalms 27:9.) He is eternally good and eternally kind. He is and has always been my dearest friend. Even in the darkest times of my life when I couldn't feel His presence and His voice was indiscernible, He was there with me.

One of those dark times in my life was in June 2009 when I lost Pam, my precious wife of 40 years. She was a wonderful wife and friend and an incredible mom. After her death, I went through what is known as the dark night of the soul—much like the widow of Nain.

Several weeks after her death, I took a cruise on the Caribbean Sea. One night as I was standing outside my room on the balcony, gazing into the starry skies and the dark waters, I found myself thinking I didn't want to live anymore. I imagined what it would be like to jump off into the dark night waters. No one was around, and I would be gone before anyone became aware of my plight. Just like that poor widow woman, I was in the depths of despair, hopeless and without purpose—or so I thought. In that moment of desperation, the One I have loved all these years was present. In that desperate hour, moved by compassion, the Father sent His angels to guard and protect me.

Through the weeks and months ahead, Father would come to me with great compassion and love, restoring my heart, my vision, and my purpose. Then in His lovingkindness, He brought to me His unique and precious daughter Donna. We married almost two years after Pam's death, and she is the joy of my heart!

I don't know what brokenness you may have faced, what pain or loss, but I do know that the One who is compassionate is always there for you. He will bring hope where you have lost hope. He will bind up your broken heart, releasing new life, vision, and purpose into your life as He has mine. You are His beloved child and He is your Father.

Years ago, we lived in the northern part of England in an area where sheep were raised. In the spring of the year, everywhere you looked there were newborn lambs frolicking in the fresh spring weather. They ran and played—their bodies leaping straight up as if catapulted by little springs in their legs. They were such fun to watch. But sheep must be continually led to green pastures as they exhaust the grass in one area, and they must be watered by still, calm water; if not, they will run away.

As Jesus walked among the multitudes, He viewed them as weary and scattered sheep that had been abused by the ravages of life, and He was moved with compassion. Compassion and kindness encompass mercy; these attributes of God were constantly revealed through the life of Jesus, flowing out of the heart of His eternal love.

CHAPTER 8

MERCY

Without a revelation of the Father's mercy, you and I will become workers for God instead of beloved children of God.

The term mercy may designate both character and actions that emerge as a consequence of that character. As a part of character, mercy is demonstrated most clearly by such qualities as compassion and forbearance (patience). With respect to action an act of mercy issues from compassion and forbearance; in a legal sense mercy may involve such acts as pardon, forgiveness, or the mitigation of penalties. [12]

The Prophet Micah said:

With what shall I come before the Lord, And bow myself before the High God? Shall I come before Him with burnt offerings, With calves a year old? Will the Lord be pleased with thousands of rams, Ten thousand rivers of oil? Shall I give my firstborn for my transgression, The fruit of my body for the sin of my soul? (Mic. 6:6-7)

Over the years, I have known very gifted and talented believers who desperately desired to know the Father but were unable to comprehend His mercy for them. I believe their views of the Heavenly Father were marred as a result of their relationships with their earthly fathers. If you asked them if God were merciful, they would say, "Absolutely!" but they were unable to experience mercy in their own lives. As a result, they would continue to do good works as a means to please man and God in order to gain approval and validation. They would set their minds on a goal but every time they would approach it, it would move further out of their reach.

⊰⊰⊱⊰

Daniel's Testimony
(The name has been changed to protect his privacy.)

Daniel is a young man from a traditional Asian family. His mother was his emotional companion. His father was a strict, patriarchal figure who worked very hard to provide for them; he had very little patience and would get angry at the slightest provocation. These actions led to many embarrassing moments. *"I can remember wanting to disassociate myself from him…."* Vowing that he would never be like his father, Daniel suppressed his feelings and emotions.

His father was never interested in what he had to say and showed favoritism to his younger sister, causing Daniel to resent him even more. Furthermore, Daniel's father thought that he was always right and everybody else was always wrong. There were times of physical discipline, and though that was very painful, the greatest pain Daniel suffered was from a wounded heart, inflicted by the very hands that should have nurtured and protected him. "I would refuse to cry because I didn't want to show weakness. In fact, I would often challenge him to hit me longer and harder as if mocking his physical exertions. But I would cry afterwards in my room … trembling with rage and injustice, hot tears streaming down my cheeks…. The distance and coldness grew like a great chasm that neither of us wanted to bridge…. I simply refused to talk to him and erected a wall between us."

Daniel received Christ at the age of ten. He spoke of the love of the Father but, in his heart, "God was more like a godfather than God the Father because of the way that fatherhood was modeled to me by my earthly father."

"So who is Father God? And what is the Father's heart? For twenty years as a Christian and believer it was something that I could not fathom. And it was something I didn't even realize I needed to know. God chose to reveal His Father's heart to me…. In the midst of an impending divorce, all my misconceptions of Father God were brought to the surface.

"I returned from a mission trip to the biggest shock of my life. My wife revealed her secret past to me which completely rocked my world and challenged what I thought her to be—a God-loving, God-fearing woman. How could it be? This was the woman I had been in love with for nine years! She told me that she was in love with another man. In the space of one week, my marriage became a huge flaming wreck and I was scrambling to put out the fires that engulfed both of us.

"I had just returned from serving God! …I have been serving Him faithfully, teaching Sunday school, playing the piano during church service, leading Bible discussions, and going on mission trips. I appeared to be the model Christian and God should never have allowed such a thing to happen! In performing so many tasks well, I thought I would be able to score some brownie points with Him. But Father God had diagnosed my heart condition. It wasn't about serving Him; it was all about putting on a show for man to see. He had to nail my spirit of performance. He wasn't interested in all the things that I could do and how well I could perform them. He was more interested in a heart-to-heart relationship, and He wanted all these things to be an overflow of a connectedness with Him!

"All the while, I had been doing these things with murmuring and complaining— never with gladness of heart. As a porn addict, I was living a double life myself. I never gave love and affection to my wife, and the trust between us had been broken ever since she had discovered my secret porn addiction. In many ways, I had become like my father; the very man I vowed never to become.

"So when the crisis hit, it seemed as if God were punishing me. Seeing myself as a rotten, wretched, and sinful man, I opened myself up to receive this punishment that I knew I so greatly deserved. I confessed my sin repeatedly to people who would bother to listen, and I conceded that my marriage was over and that I didn't deserve God's love or my wife's love. The only model that I had was that of my father and the punishment that I had received from his hands since I was young. Because of that, I thought that Father God must be punishing me as well. The Bible says that He's a judge, so I surmised that He was judging me for my sins.

"The good news is that He wouldn't allow me to stay there. As I began to spend quality time with Him in prayer and communication, my misconception of Him began to change."

As Daniel began to meditate on the Word of God, He began to discern the lies of the enemy and to understand what was really on the heart of his Heavenly Father. "The truth is, Father God was heartbroken at my waywardness, yet He still loved me so much. He desired to address all the root issues that were gnawing at my marriage, especially the issue of my self-identity as a child of God. He needed me to rediscover my joy, my voice, my destiny and purpose, and to rebuild a marriage around that, on a firm foundation that cannot be shaken. The only way He could do that was to take it completely apart before He could put it back together again.

"All the while, He kept telling me that I'm His dearly beloved son. He put so many signposts in my life showing me that He is always around, that He cares, and that He was never mad at me—a verse from a devotional, a song on the radio, a phone call from a friend. Every 'random' thing was God showing me that He's always in a good mood!

"In the days, weeks, and months of crisis management that followed, I prayed like I have never prayed before. I'd spend much time on my knees praying and weeping into my tear-soaked chair. Sometimes I would even fall asleep halfway through. Nothing seemed to be happening, and I would get so upset at myself for not enduring through my tiredness and staying awake a little bit longer to pray that little bit more! I came to realize that Father God was concerned about my physical, mental, and emotional exhaustion so that He gave me rest even as I was spending time with Him in prayer. What I wanted to pray, He already knew. It wasn't about praying long and flowery prayers. He just wanted to capture my heart, as a Father does his child, and His touch was so reassuring and tender that I would fall asleep in the midst of prayer with Him.

"It took some time, and many months of tears and pain. Miraculously, Father God restored my marriage. I have always heard other people's testimonies about how Father God is able to redeem and restore the broken-hearted unto Himself, yet I never saw myself as that someone special who deserved such extravagant love.

"But now, I understand for myself His nature. He binds the broken-hearted and sets the captives free. He comforts those who mourn and grieve. He bestows a crown of beauty instead of ashes, the oil of joy instead of mourning, and a garment of praise instead of a spirit of despair. The Father's love is for everyone! A true understanding of the Father heart of God was birthed even in the midst of the storm. I'm so overjoyed not only to be born again, but also to enjoy the fruit of a relationship with Him that is born again. I'm so happy that He is my Father, and I am His son, and that every child is special to Him!"

࿔࿔࿔࿔

My wife Donna and I know this young man personally and have seen the incredible fruit in his life and in his wife. This is a glorious testimony to the amazing love and mercy of the Father.

Some of us can certainly identify with Daniel's statement, "I never saw myself as that someone special who deserved such extravagant love." But extravagant love is what defines the Father.

Just as the father in the prodigal son story, Father God waits patiently for us to surrender to Him all our pain, shame, and worry. He waits to embrace us with His unfailing love; to extend to us his mercy. The "*great sadness*," as Paul Young calls it, deep within the recesses of our heart cannot be healed without Him. We cannot perform enough to rid ourselves of the ravages of life that have so hindered us and our destiny, but God can remove these hindrances and desires to do so.

When we mess up, we think: "I've got to be good; I'll do better." But that only serves to reinforce the belief system that we are bad. The Father tells us we can't do it alone—we have to let Him do it for us.

All that the Father desires is our heart. We must be willing to be transparent with Him, allowing Him to reveal the cause of our pain and then heal it as He did with Daniel. Then, and only then, can we come into the incredible relationship with Him that He so desires.

In Mark 10:17, we find the story of a rich, young ruler who came to Jesus desiring to know what he could do to obtain eternal life. Much like Daniel, he had been performing all of his life in order to merit God's approval. He was really asking what he could do in order to earn eternal life on his own. This young man had kept the Ten Commandments all of his life; the thing he lacked was total commitment to God.

Jesus told him to sell whatever he had and give to the poor, then take up his cross, and follow Him. The young man was filled with great sorrow because he had great possessions, which had become his idol. Through his works, he had received approval and validation from man, and he was unwilling to lay down those things—with their accompanying praise and honor—for fear of losing his identity. Jesus wanted to free him to walk in the destiny that God had for him from the foundation of the world.

We have all been there. We hide behind a mask and continue to perform in order to gain favor with God. But we have already obtained that favor the day we received Jesus Christ as our Lord and Savior. God's favor has *never* depended on what we can give Him but on what He has already given us through the Cross. When we embrace this truth, we are able to come into the liberty and freedom Christ intends for us. It is then that we come to the revelation that we are not orphans but beloved sons and daughters of God—adopted into His wonderful family and heirs of our eternal loving Father.

Justice

God's justice expressed in an individual's life is for the sole purpose of restoring that which has been damaged by this world.

> *"Behold! My Servant whom I uphold, My Elect One in whom My soul delights! I have put My Spirit upon Him; He will bring forth justice to the Gentiles. He will not cry out, nor raise His voice, Nor cause His voice to be heard in the street. A bruised reed He will not break, And smoking flax He will not quench; He will bring forth justice for truth. He will not fail nor be discouraged, Till He has established justice in the earth; And the coastlands shall wait for His law." (Is. 42:1-4)*

In Luke 13, we observe Jesus bringing justice to a woman who has been bent over for eighteen years as a result of a spirit of infirmity. Not only had she suffered physical pain, but think of the incredible humiliation she must have suffered as well.

> *Now He was teaching in one of the synagogues on the Sabbath. And behold, there was a woman who had a spirit of infirmity eighteen years, and was bent over and could in no way raise herself up. But when Jesus saw her, He called her to Him and said to her, "Woman, you are loosed from your infirmity." And He laid His hands on her, and immediately she was made straight, and glorified God.*

> *But the ruler of the synagogue answered with indignation, because Jesus had healed on the Sabbath; and he said to the crowd, "There are six days on which men ought to work; therefore come and be healed on them, and not on the Sabbath day."*

> *The Lord then answered him and said, "Hypocrite! Does not each one of you on the Sabbath loose his ox or donkey from the stall, and lead it away to water it? So ought not this woman, being a daughter of Abraham, whom Satan has bound—think of it—for eighteen years, be loosed from*

*this bond on the Sabbath?" And when He said these things,
all His adversaries were put to shame; and all the multitude
rejoiced for all the glorious things that were done by Him.
(Luke 13:10-17)*

Jesus saw this woman as He was teaching and His
heart was gripped with compassion for her. He called her
to Him and laid His hands on her saying, *"Woman you are
loosed from your infirmity."* Immediately, she was restored.
For the first time in eighteen years, she was able to stand
straight and tall as in the days of her youth. Imagine what
those around must have felt as they witnessed Jesus healing this woman they had seen bent over all these years.
They must have been spellbound.

But the leaders of the synagogue were incensed and
challenged Him with the Law, *"There are six days on which
men ought to work; therefore come and be healed on them,
and not on the Sabbath day."*

Can you imagine what the people watching must have
been thinking? "You've got to be kidding! A great miracle
has just happened before our very eyes, and you are ob-
jecting because of the Law?"

Jesus didn't mince words. He called the leaders hyp-
ocrites! He pointed out that his adversaries would treat
their livestock better than this woman. After eighteen
years, didn't she deserve to be set free? After all, she was a
daughter of Abraham!

Justice was served that day, bringing restoration to
the woman's crooked body. His justice would also expose
truth about the lies that the leaders had believed regarding a loving, compassionate Father. The justice of God always takes those things that are bent and returns them to
their original design.

Like this woman, we can be bent from the lies of the
evil one; bent beneath the hidden pain that we have

carried all of our lives. Made in the image of God with His nature and character as part of our DNA, we were created with great nobility and dignity. But the enemy has stolen much of this through the lies and wounds that he has inflicted upon us throughout our lives. For each of us, the Father comes to bring justice to those places where we have been damaged, in order to restore us to our original design. He calls us even now as we read these words to come to Him. He alone is able to restore those damaged places in our lives.

> …*God anointed Jesus of Nazareth with the Holy Spirit and with power, who went about doing good and healing all who were oppressed by the devil, for God was with Him. (Acts 10:38)*

This is an incredible revelation of truth. Take time to meditate on these words so you don't miss it. Remember that everything that Jesus spoke and did was a complete revelation of the heart of God for all humanity. The Father's heart is fully engaged in each of our lives moment by moment, day by day, and His desire is for your good.

The Blind Can See

Let's look at an encounter that Jesus had with a man who had been born blind. Jesus had just left the temple where the Pharisees had attempted to stone Him for declaring to them that "'before Abraham was, I AM'" (John 8:58). As He went, He encountered a man who was born blind.

> *Now as Jesus passed by, He saw a man who was blind from birth. And His disciples asked Him, saying, "Rabbi, who sinned, this man or his parents, that he was born blind?"*

> *Jesus answered, "Neither this man nor his parents sinned, but that the works of God should be revealed in him. I must*

work the works of Him who sent Me while it is day; the night is coming when no one can work. As long as I am in the world, I am the light of the world." When He had said these things, He spat on the ground and made clay with the saliva; and He anointed the eyes of the blind man with the clay. And He said to him, "Go, wash in the pool of Siloam" (which is translated, Sent). So he went and washed, and came back seeing. (John 9:1-7)

You can just imagine what is going on in the minds of the Pharisees. They couldn't contest the miracle, for there were many witnesses to the blind man's healing. As they attempted to solve this mystery, they were also faced with the fact that Jesus had healed this man on the Sabbath, which was against their laws— although apparently it wasn't against God's law.

Consider what it must have been like for this man who was born blind. He had been limited in what he could do and where he could go. He could well have been weighed down by hopelessness. It was popular Hebrew theology at that time that blindness was a punishment from God for sin or defilement. He may have been looked down on or shunned by some. He probably wondered if anybody cared or if God cared. As a matter of fact, he must have wondered if God even knew that he existed.

Just think, here is one man out of 200 million individuals who occupied the earth at the time of Christ, and God personally encountered him. God knows each of us completely and understands all the things that concern us. He is omniscient (all knowing) but intimately involved in every detail of our lives. He desires to help us as a loving Father.

...O Lord, You have searched me and known me. You know my sitting down and my rising up; You understand my thought afar off. You comprehend my path and my lying down, and are acquainted with all my ways. (Ps. 139:1-3)

Through His encounter with the blind man, Jesus communicated the love of God, healing the man of blindness and revealing the Father's mercy, justice, and kindness to all who were witnesses that day. This broke the stronghold of the lie that blindness was a punishment from God for sin. The Lord used the healing of this man's physical sight in order to teach a spiritual truth—not only to the Pharisees, but to us as well.

Mankind's eyes have also been blinded to the truth of who our Father is and how He sees us. The Holy Spirit wants to personally reveal to us more and more of the infinite facets of the nature and character of our Heavenly Father through these encounters. Remember, the encounters Jesus had with individuals, the stories He told, and the parables He shared were for the purpose of revealing the heart of the Father to us.

Have you been blinded by the lies of the enemy, and do you know what caused that blindness? Was it from the wounds you suffered as a child or the lies the enemy spoke to you through those you trusted? One such example I remember was from an experience in tenth grade when a respected teacher called me a fool in front of my friends. His comments only deteriorated my own personal view of myself—further clouding my view of God.

The Father desires to open our eyes. If we allow Him, He will do so; however, we must be willing to let Him. We cannot do it by ourselves. We need to allow Him to apply the healing balm of His Spirit to our eyes, washing them in the water of His Word. We have to break our agreement with the lies that the enemy has spoken over us and come into agreement instead with His word. For our agreement—whether it is to the truth or to a lie—empowers its effect in our lives.

Think about what this man must have experienced as his eyes were opened to a world that he had never seen before. Imagine if you had lived in darkness all of your life and suddenly you could see for the first time what the people around you actually looked like. Suddenly you could see trees, flowers, butterflies, birds, and little children playing for the first time. It must have been a wonderful experience! The darkness that had been his familiar surrounding was now gone and there was light. The Light of the World had come and miraculously healed him.

Similarly, God desires to come to our places of darkness, to those things that have become so familiar but, in fact, are enemies trying to overtake and destroy our destinies. He desires to heal and set us free so we can see who He truly is and who we are in Him.

> Then Jesus spoke to them again, saying, "I am the light of the world. He who follows Me shall not walk in darkness, but have the light of life." (John 8:12)

You may have discovered that your vision (much like mine) isn't 20/20, having been affected at times by the lies of the evil one. Lies about our Heavenly Father have blinded our eyes to whom He truly is, thus impacting how we view ourselves. We are like this man who was born blind, but we have experienced *spiritual* blindness and, because of this, haven't clearly seen the Light of Life.

God wants to open our eyes also and give us new sight. Where we have been damaged, He will bring His justice in order to restore what has been bent to its original design. A loving, merciful Father, our God tenderly cares for each of us who are made in His image.

CHAPTER 9

A BRUISED REED

A bruised reed He will not break, And smoking flax He will not quench; He will bring forth justice for truth. (Is. 42:3)

We have some good friends whose greatest passion in life is to share the love of the Father with those whom the world would see as the least—the outcasts of society. Janet was raised in a home that wasn't safe. An abusive alcoholic, her father gambled away any money that he earned, causing her family great poverty, rejection, and physical pain. Their home was a shack, containing very few material goods.

Once when she was a little child, there was no food in the house, and someone brought them boxes of food. It was like Christmas morning. She spent time looking at each can of food and thinking, "One day I want to help those, like myself, who have nothing."

Janet's Testimony
(The name has been changed to protect her privacy.)

I grew up with an alcoholic, abusive father. At the age of five, he told me that he was going to kill me. I believed him. I tried to hold back the tears but was unsuccessful, which only made him angrier. I curled into a little ball and prayed my first prayer, asking God to make me stop crying so I wouldn't get hit. Instantly, I felt Someone pick me up and rock me. I knew this Someone was God. I felt a love that can't be described. He held me close and soothed my fearful heart. I fell in love. From that point on, I pursued this Father God. He was my everything.

When I would get beaten or sexually abused or yelled at, I would run to Him, and He was always there, waiting to comfort me. I lived in two worlds—one that was dark and filled with pain and terror and the other that was filled with light and love and peace—so much peace. I met Jesus when I was twelve and gave my life to Him as my Savior. The abuse continued, but it only drove me deeper into my relationship with God and His Son. He had become everything to me.

At age sixteen, I was raped by my boss. For the first time in my life, I chose not to turn to God. I turned away and ran as fast as I could. Thankfully, our Heavenly Father is faithful even when we aren't. He refused to give up on me but pursued me relentlessly. He would whisper how much He missed me or show up in my dreams or speak to me through Scripture, but I refused to listen. Two painful years later, I fell on my knees and asked God to forgive me. He swept over me like a tidal wave of pure love and said, "I've missed you, and I still love you! Welcome home!"

Oh, what a kind, loving Father we have! He never gives up on us and His love never fails! He really can make beautiful things out of dust.

⊰⊰⊱⊱

Years later, Janet met the love of her life; for years they carried in their hearts a dream to have a retreat center where they could invite those who were broken, wounded, abused, and without hope. Their desire was to partner with the Lord in healing and setting free those who were made in His image. Six years ago, they saw their dream come true. Today, on over 300 acres of beautiful rolling land, they have established a quiet place where broken ones can come and be healed.

One by one those who have been damaged by the world are healed and those without hope begin to discover their destiny. Broken lives, the "bruised reeds" and "smoking flax" we read about in Isaiah 42:3, experience the justice of God at the Farm. He takes those things that have been bent and restores them to their original design. They come as spiritual orphans—beaten, wounded, and bruised—and leave as beloved sons and daughters of the Father.

Janet Continues Her Story

Our Father's Farm was a dream that began on our honeymoon on October 17, 1976, when we discovered a shared desire to bring healing and hope to women and children in crisis. We joined hands and committed to pray until the day God would bring it to pass. During the 30 years of prayer and waiting, we were being trained to effectively demonstrate unconditional love to those who are devastated.

On October 17, 2007, (exactly 31 years to the day) we purchased a 347-acre farm, which is dedicated to ministering the love of the Father. In less than five years, the Lord provided the finances to build eight ministry homes plus a 20,000 square foot building dedicated to training and providing homes for girls rescued from sex trafficking. We've asked the Lord to send us those who are considered hopeless by the world because we understand that His love is enough and love never fails.

One thing I love about God is that He never withholds His love but pours it out on everyone—even His enemies! It's a free gift; all we have to do is receive it. Our Father's

Farm is a manifestation on the earth of the exceedingly abundant, extravagant, lavish nature of God's love for weak, broken people. He loves well—perfectly, and without regret. His love can and does transform the most shattered hearts, and I am living proof!

Shame desires a covering, so Jesus became that covering for each one who receives Him as Lord and Savior. "At the cross Jesus willingly traded His life for ours and it stands as immutable evidence of His love for us." [13]

Even when we come into the kingdom of God, shame can cause us to run away from God, instead of to Him. It is a horrible accuser, attacking our minds with tormenting lies. If we agree with those lies, we will end up accusing ourselves daily of things from our past from which the blood of Jesus has already cleansed us. Not only have we been forgiven totally of our sins, but since *"there is therefore now no condemnation to those who are in Christ Jesus…"* (Rom. 8:1), we can also stand with clear consciences.

> *How much more shall the blood of Christ, who through the eternal Spirit offered Himself without spot to God, cleanse your conscience from dead works to serve the living God? (Heb. 9:14)*

This is wonderful news! We don't have to allow the enemy to accuse us any longer from that which the blood of Jesus has already cleansed us. We are new creations in Christ and all things have become new!

The Woman Caught in Adultery

As we continue on our journey, we meet a woman who was once an outcast—rejected by her family and society—but now is the beloved daughter of our Father. How could such a tremendous change take place?

Then the scribes and Pharisees brought to Him a woman caught in adultery. And when they had set her in the midst, they said to Him, "Teacher, this woman was caught in adultery, in the very act. Now Moses, in the law, commanded us that such should be stoned. But what do You say?" This they said, testing Him, that they might have something of which to accuse Him. But Jesus stooped down and wrote on the ground with His finger, as though He did not hear.

So when they continued asking Him, He raised Himself up and said to them, "He who is without sin among you, let him throw a stone at her first." And again He stooped down and wrote on the ground.

Then those who heard it, being convicted by their conscience, went out one by one, beginning with the oldest even to the last. And Jesus was left alone, and the woman standing in the midst. When Jesus had raised Himself up and saw no one but the woman, He said to her, "Woman, where are those accusers of yours? Has no one condemned you?"

She said, "No one, Lord."

And Jesus said to her, "Neither do I condemn you; go and sin no more." (John 8:3-11)

Consider the scribes and Pharisees in this story. Jesus was not only concerned about the young woman but also about these religious zealots—He is always concerned for the hearts of men. God is *"…not willing that any should perish but that all should come to repentance" (2 Pet. 3:9).* He wants all of mankind to come to the saving knowledge of Jesus; to be free and reconciled to the Father through the finished work of the Cross.

The men in this story had one motive and that was to ensnare Jesus in some wrongdoing in order to accuse

Him. *"Teacher, this woman was caught in adultery, in the very act. Now Moses, in the law, commanded us that such should be stoned. But what do You say?"* They quoted the law correctly, and accordingly, this woman should die; however, God had a higher purpose.

Jesus responded to her accusers, *"He who is without sin among you, let him throw a stone at her first."* It is interesting that He didn't stand there and stare these men down, shaming them into doing the right thing. He simply made the statement and stooped back down to draw in the dirt, letting their own consciences convict them. Caught in their own trap, one by one they quietly slipped away from the One who could set them free, leaving Him there with the woman they had condemned.

> For God did not send His Son into the world to condemn the world, but that the world through Him might be saved. (John 3:17)

Her death that day would not be a physical death at their hands. She would lay down her life by her own free will as she received Jesus and His forgiveness and died to her sins.

> I have been crucified with Christ; it is no longer I who live, but Christ lives in me; and the life which I now live in the flesh I live by faith in the Son of God, who loved me and gave Himself for me. (Gal. 2:20)

> Therefore, if anyone is in Christ, he is a new creation; old things have passed away; behold, all things have become new. (2 Cor. 5:17)

The Woman's Perspective

Imagine with me the woman standing there before Jesus and listen to *her* story:

"I had heard of Him; in fact, I had seen Him from time to time, but I didn't know Him. They called Him Master and Teacher. Some had even declared that He was the Messiah. All around me men were demanding loudly, *'So what do you say we should do to her, Master? She was caught in the very act of adultery.'*

"Shame overwhelmed me and I hung my head. Though I fought hard to hold them back, tears spilled over and ran down my face.

"And where is the man who not moments ago was with me; what about him? I wanted to cry out, but I dared not utter the desperate words audibly.

"The Pharisees clearly knew what the law said, and they wanted nothing more than to trap Jesus. At the time, I didn't understand what was going on but later I realized that a religious spirit was launching its attack through these scribes and Pharisees. They were not concerned about me or the outcome, but only a way to rid themselves of this carpenter, Jesus, who had turned their whole world upside down. *'So tell us, what does the law say?'* they demanded.

"I found myself watching the One they called Teacher. He had knelt down and was writing something on the ground. The men surrounding me were demanding a response, and yet this man was simply writing on the ground, seemingly unaware of what was going on around Him."

It is not hard to imagine the kind of life that led this woman to her present-day circumstances. Her story might mirror that of many young women today:

"My mind turned back to the time when I was a child. Our father had left home when I was very young. All I can remember about my father is his ranting and yelling and my mother's tears. Our home was filled with anger; it was not like the Rabbis taught, but was one of constant turmoil. I remembered some of my friends' fathers who were loving and kind and how my heart yearned for a father's affection—I longed for a father who would hold, love, and encourage me; a loving father who would be there when I just needed to talk. I longed for a father who would protect me and tuck me in at night.

"I had this deep hunger for approval and validation; my quest to fill the emptiness in my heart led me to numerous relationships with men, as I desperately sought the love I so desired. Finally it had brought me to this place. They called me a woman of the night—a harlot. Desiring a father's love, I had given myself over and over again to men who would tell me what I longed to hear. But in the end, they only used me for their own needs, eventually leaving me again empty-hearted. Pain filled my heart and I thought I would never find the one thing I so longed for—a father's love.

"Once again, the voices of the religious zealots fill the air pulling me to the present, *'What do you say, Jesus? The law says she is to be stoned.'*

"Terror fills my heart and I think: The day has finally come when I will pay for my actions. Today I will die and the desire I so long for will never be fulfilled. But this is no less than I deserve.

"And then I hear His voice, *'He who is without sin among you, let him throw a stone at her first.'* I cringe, waiting for the first stone to batter my body.

"They stand stunned as if hit by an unseen force. Moments before, everything was chaos, but now a leaden silence has descended over the crowd.

"One by one, the very ones who wanted me dead turn and walk away. Left alone with this man, I continue to stare at the ground. And then He speaks in His still, quiet voice, *'Woman, where are those accusers of yours? Has no one condemned you?'*

"*Lifting my eyes, I turn to look around, and then I look full into His face, and at that moment I find myself gazing into the eyes of the* Author of Love. Suddenly, somewhere deep inside my heart, the hardness begins to break, the chains snap, and my heart begins to fill with warmth. I hear myself saying, *'No one, Lord.'*

'Neither do I condemn you; go and sin no more.'

"Moments ago there was a crowd of men wanting to stone me, but now Jesus was saying He didn't condemn me. What can this mean? I know I am guilty! If He is saying I'm forgiven, then who is He? Only God can forgive, but still He said, *'…go and sin no more.'*

"He respectfully called me woman, not harlot. My heart turns toward Him. It is like a father correcting me, yet oh, so lovingly…telling me not to be caught in this again. He is giving me another chance. The chains of shame and the shackles of sin fall from my heart, and I am inexplicably drawn to Him. It is not like with the other men. I have never known a man like this. As I look upon Him, I begin to see the heart of the Father. The more I look, the more my heart is transformed. I begin to see, if but dimly, how He sees me—not as an adulterer or a harlot—but as a daughter and as a part of the bride of Christ, for this day He has given me salvation."

"Neither do I condemn you; go and sin no more." This is the power of love that transforms our hearts.

Can you imagine how this woman's life was changed after her encounter with Jesus? She could never be the same. In an instant, the Holy Spirit broke the chains from her heart, setting her free. Once, she was a prisoner without hope, but Jesus set her free. The eyes of her heart were opened, and she saw the Father for the first time.

Her heart was gripped by a love that she had searched for her entire life and she was filled with joy and peace. She would no longer be an orphan but would forever be the daughter of the Most-High God.

No matter where you have been or what you have done, open your heart to Jesus and allow His Spirit to set you free—free to be all that the Father has destined you to be. The woman was brought to this place by others, and in the midst of the turmoil going on around her, God encountered her, not with condemnation, judgment, or anger but with mercy and forgiveness. Shame no longer defined her—she was no longer a woman of the night.

Don't allow shame to hold you prisoner. Come to Jesus. He is here right now to meet you, not with condemnation but with forgiveness. He has heard your cries and seen your tears. His arms are outstretched, welcoming you to come and lay down all that has held you captive—all that has caused deep pain in your life. Come and rest in His embrace and allow Him to heal and restore you. He is a safe haven, and it is here you will discover His love and who He truly is through His Son.

CHAPTER 10

THE REDEMPTIVE GRACE OF GOD

He Rebuilds Us

> *The Lord has appeared of old to me, saying: "Yes, I have loved you with an everlasting love; Therefore with loving kindness I have drawn you. Again I will build you, and you shall be rebuilt, O virgin of Israel! You shall again be adorned with your tambourines, And shall go forth in the dances of those who rejoice. (Jer. 31:3-4)*

Oh, how my heart leaps for joy when I read this text. The prophet is speaking to *us* as well as to Israel. He is speaking of the nature and character of God and of His everlasting lovingkindness that is for everyone. God is the One who first loved us and chose us, out of His eternal love and kindness. God has never *needed* anything, but He deeply desires that we know Him.

> *And this is eternal life, that they may know You, the only true God, and Jesus Christ whom You have sent. (John 17:3)*

To know Him is to encounter and experience Him at the deepest level of relationship. Jeremiah 31:4 states, *"I will rebuild you..."* The heart of the Father is to reestablish all who come to Him through Christ.

> *"The Spirit of the Lord God is upon Me, because the Lord has anointed Me to preach good tidings to the poor; He has sent Me to heal the brokenhearted, to proclaim liberty to the*

captives, and the opening of the prison to those who are bound; to proclaim the acceptable year of the Lord, and the day of vengeance of our God; to comfort all who mourn, to console those who mourn in Zion, to give them beauty for ashes, the oil of joy for mourning, the garment of praise for the spirit of heaviness; that they may be called trees of righteousness, the planting of the Lord, that He may be glorified." (Is. 61:1-3)

He wants to restore us spiritually, emotionally, and physically. No matter where you are or where you have been, the Father desires relationship with you. You are special; never in all creation has there been anyone like you. You are unique, and though the ravages of this world may have had some negative impact on you, if you allow Him, He will straighten out those places in your life that have been bent.

The Woman at the Well

Many of us are familiar with the story found in John 4:5-26 of Jesus meeting the Samaritan woman at the city well. His disciples had gone to purchase food in town, and Jesus sat down by a well to rest. As He sat there, a woman of the city approached to draw water, and Jesus asked her for a drink.

The Jews viewed Samaritans as outcasts. Originally Israelites, the Samaritans had married into the foreign families that had been sent by the Assyrians and Babylonians to occupy Palestine. In the region of Samaria where they lived, they had their own version of the Law of Moses. Instead of worshiping at the temple in Jerusalem, they had built their own temple on Mount Gerizim and had their own priesthood. They claimed belief in the God of Israel and the laws of Torah while worshiping the gods of the foreign settlers with whom they had blended. Neither the race nor the religion was pure. The Jews had nothing to do with the Samaritans; yet, here Jesus was requesting a Samaritan to give Him a drink.

Taken aback, the woman responded, *"How is it that You, being a Jew, ask a drink from me, a Samaritan woman?"*

Jesus answered, *"If you knew the gift of God, and who it is who says to you, 'Give Me a drink,' you would have asked Him, and He would have given you living water."*

She replied, *"Sir, You have nothing to draw with, and the well is deep. Where then do You get that living water?"*

Jesus declared, *"Whoever drinks of this water will thirst again, but whoever drinks of the water that I shall give him will never thirst. But the water that I shall give him will become in him a fountain of water springing up into everlasting life."*

This Samaritan woman is standing at the well in the heat of the day. Every day she comes to the same well to draw water to carry back to the city, and here is a man telling her that He has water that will satisfy her so that she will never thirst again.

This surely piqued her interest. *"Sir, give me this water that I may not thirst, nor come here to draw."*

Jesus had her full attention now and told her, *"Go, call your husband, and come here."*

"I have no husband," she replied.

To this response, the Holy Spirit gave Jesus revelation, and He said, *"You have well said, 'I have no husband,' for you have had five husbands, and the one whom you now have is not your husband; in that, you spoke truly."*

At this point, we get a glimpse into the Father's heart. The heart of the Father is never to condemn us but to save us and set us free. The word of knowledge Jesus speaks is not meant in condemnation but to awaken her heart to truth.

"Sir, I perceive that You are a prophet. Our fathers worshiped on this mountain, and you Jews say that in Jerusalem is the place where one ought to worship."

She had heard the truth and it pierced her heart. She longed to believe, but she is not sure if she can trust Him. Religion has misled her, people have lied to her, and life has been hard.

Jesus replied, *"Woman, believe Me, the hour is coming when you will neither on this mountain, nor in Jerusalem, worship the Father. You worship what you do not know; we know what we worship, for salvation is of the Jews. But the hour is coming, and now is, when the true worshipers will worship the Father in spirit and truth; for the Father is seeking such to worship Him. God is Spirit, and those who worship Him must worship in spirit and truth."*

Her heart comes alive within her and she realizes this man is safe as she says to Him, *"I know that Messiah is coming"* (who is called Christ). *"When He comes, He will tell us all things."* At this point she is sharing her deepest desire. She wants to know the truth, to be free, and to be truly loved.

And then Jesus said to her, *"I who speak to you am He."* He was telling her He was the One she had heard of and had searched for all of her life. He was the One with the answers!

Many of us have such a misconception of the heart of the Father. We see Him as sitting in heaven just waiting for an opportunity to strike us down. It is such a lie! He doesn't do that. His truth that issues forth out of a heart of unconditional love brings conviction for the purpose of setting us free.

Moments earlier, this woman was about her daily chore of getting water, only to be confronted by the Author of Love. Met head-on with truth, her heart was captured by His love and she was changed. She went immediately to tell everyone who would listen; the Word says many of the Samaritans believed in Jesus because of her testimony. And many more believed because of His own testimony when they heard Him for themselves.

They told the woman, *"Now we believe, not because of what you said, for we ourselves have heard Him and we know that this is indeed the Christ the Savior of the world."*

God Pursues Us

Afraid of not doing everything right and offending God, I ended up performing instead of just being who He created me to be—His son—the one He loves unconditionally. He has promised that He will complete the work begun in me. My only responsibility is to trust Him and rest in what He has done. Anne also thought she had to perform, but the Lord proved differently to her as well. She thought that like her earthly father, God would punish her for her failures or mistakes in life, but He just kept pursuing her.

Anne's Testimony
(The name has been changed to protect her privacy.)

If I did not perform well in school or my mum caught me playing on the computer, my dad would use clothes hangers and cane me on my arms.

Father has never punished me into obedience toward Him all these years. He has always been that loving, kind-hearted, faithful, gentle Father who poured out His love towards me and whispered a gentle whisper to me if I should stray away slightly. He never stops pursuing me, wooing me, and chasing me. This is what our Heavenly Father's heart really is.

ॐॐॐॐ

Levi Experiences God's Grace

Then He went out again by the sea; and all the multitude came to Him, and He taught them. As He passed by, He saw Levi the son of Alphaeus sitting at the tax office. And He said to him, "Follow Me." So he arose and followed Him. Now it happened, as He was dining in Levi's house that many tax collectors and sinners also sat together with Jesus and His disciples; for there were many, and they followed Him.

And when the scribes and Pharisees saw Him eating with the tax collectors and sinners, they said to His disciples, "How is it that He eats and drinks with tax collectors and sinners?" When Jesus heard it, He said to them,

"Those who are well have no need of a physician, but those who are sick. I did not come to call the righteous, but sinners, to repentance." (Mark 2:13-17)

Jesus said He had come to save the lost, and that meant everyone—even tax collectors. Society probably hated Levi. Tax collectors were not well-liked because of the typically dishonest way that they performed their duties—taking far more than what was owed. Yet, here is Jesus inviting Levi to follow Him, then going to His house for a meal, joining him there with other sinners.

The Pharisees were annoyed at these actions; yet, Levi was to be one of the twelve apostles that Jesus had selected after spending a night in prayer with the Father. Maybe that surprises you, but in this story, we observe the mercy and grace of our Heavenly Father. Jesus even changed Levi's name to Matthew—which means "gift from God"—showing further how He felt about this man.

Now it came to pass in those days that He went out to the mountain to pray, and continued all night in prayer to God.

And when it was day, He called His disciples to Himself; and from them He chose twelve whom He also named apostles: (Luke 6:12-13)

Called to Be Fishers of Men

The Gospels tell of Jesus walking by the Sea of Galilee and seeing two brothers, Simon (called Peter) and Andrew, casting their net into the sea and fishing. These were two more of His chosen apostles. Jesus told them to follow Him and He would make them "fishers of men."

I have a good friend, Greg, who is an incredible lover of God. He knows that He is beloved of the Father and his relationship with God reflects His belief, but it wasn't always like this. Raised in the bayous of Louisiana, Greg spent much of his early professional years as a shrimper and drug-dealer. He was rough and hard—both in his body and in his heart. He lived for the moment, doing things that would eventually affect him physically.

One day, however, Jesus encountered Greg, mercifully revealing His love for him. He called Greg to follow Him (just as He had Peter and Andrew) and made him a fisher of men.

Greg is one of the most admirable men I know. He is a man's man, yet, he is very childlike in his faith. To hear his testimony is to experience firsthand how God can transform the hardest heart with His truth, grace, and love. Before Christ, I am certain that he was despised by many, but today, because of the grace of God working in his life, he is loved and respected as a man of integrity and a man of faith by his family, friends, and all who encounter him. It is as Paul writes:

For by grace you have been saved through faith, and that not of yourselves; it is the gift of God, not of works, lest anyone should boast. (Eph. 2:8-9)

By its simplest definition, grace is God's undeserved favor. More completely, it is God's lovingkindness being expressed in our lives as He exerts His holy influence upon us—turning us to Christ, keeping, strengthening, and maturing us in our faith, and empowering us to live our lives reflecting His nature and character.

Grace is a *gift* that flows out of the Father's unconditional love and kindness. It is totally underserved and unasked for. God in His infinite love and mercy has revealed His amazing nature to us through this gift.

When I consider where I was before Christ and where I am today, my heart is filled with gratitude for His indescribable gift to me. His grace has taken me from a little boy who felt abandoned and fatherless, to where I stand today—a beloved son. Grace has healed me from the wounds of the past and delivered me from the lies of the evil one. His grace upon my life continues to draw me to Him and influences me in such a way that I desire Him more today than when He first encountered me.

Do you see His heart? Right where you are now, let Him love you. If you will bring Him your hidden suffering, He will heal you, deliver you, and restore you. You have been born for such a time as this. You are a world changer; God wants you to change the world around you. Come by His grace and enter into His rest.

We live in a world of great demands, and though unspoken, much of the time those demands require perfection. This standard has infiltrated not only secular society but the church as well. We have been led to believe that performance is essential in order to experience God's grace and pleasure. That is such a misconception of the grace of God—His grace is unearned! God delights in giving us what we don't deserve. He pardons all of our sins and lavishes on us His goodness. He takes pleasure in giving us good gifts in order to demonstrate the glory of His kindness, love, and mercy to us and to the world.

David, the Apple of God's Eye

David wrote these words about God's grace and goodness in Psalm 40:

> *Many, O Lord my God, are Your wonderful works Which You have done; And Your thoughts toward us cannot be recounted to You in order; If I would declare and speak of them, They are more than can be numbered. (Ps. 40:5)*

Though a fierce warrior, David was also a zealous lover of God. His life reflects a man who knew who he was, what his purpose was in life, and how God viewed him. But his life was not without mistakes. In his encounter with Bathsheba, he committed adultery, lied, and murdered. Yet, in spite of these things, God loved him—not his sins, but his heart. In Psalm 51, David threw himself on the grace and mercy of God; for he knew that God, in His infinite love, would pardon him. Although he and his family suffered greatly for his sins, God declared that David was the "apple of His eye." Why would the Father say this after all of his failures? It was because of the Father's unfailing, unconditional love. David knew how to receive the grace of God and to rest in who he was in the Father's love for him.

When we make mistakes in our lives, we need to be like David and understand what grace truly is and receive the forgiveness that God has given to us in Christ. It is available to each one of us—we just have to receive it. His grace empowers you and me to become all that God has destined us to be and is always available to those who come to Him.

Let us therefore come boldly to the throne of grace that we may obtain mercy and find grace to help in time of need. (Heb. 4:16)

We see how this throne is no longer a throne of judgment for the believer, but it is a throne of grace. At the throne, we can obtain mercy (this is for our past) and grace (for our present and future). No longer under the law but under grace, we can enter into an incredible relationship with our Father where we can experience the wonder of who He truly is. Living in His presence and in the reality of His grace, our hearts will be transformed. We will no longer be influenced by the desires of the flesh, but we will be motivated by the love of God. A love for us that is unconditional and immutable—for God will never change!

The gospel of the grace of God awakens an intense longing in human souls and an equally intense resentment, because the truth that it reveals is not palatable or easy to swallow. There is a certain pride in people that causes them to give and give, but to come and accept a gift is another thing. I will give my life to martyrdom; I will dedicate my life to service; I will do anything. But do not humiliate me to the level of the most hell-deserving sinner and tell me that all I have to do is accept the gift of salvation through Jesus Christ.[14]

Every good gift and every perfect gift is from above, and comes down from the Father of lights, with whom there is no variation or shadow of turning. (Jam. 1:17

This gift of salvation, provided by the grace of God, is not just a free ticket out of hell and into heaven. It is also a gift that provides healing and deliverance to the spirit, soul, and body in order that we might be fully alive in Him. God is the source of all grace and it flows out of His infinite love for all who have been made in His image.

When I think about the cross, I picture Jesus writhing in pain. But then He sees His mother Mary as she stands watching through tears of sorrow, and He says, *"Woman, behold your son!"* and then to His beloved disciple beside her, *"Behold your mother!"* And looking upon all those who had treated Him unjustly, beaten and mocked Him, He said, *"Father, forgive them, for they do not know what they do."* It is such astounding grace!

I have experienced His grace in the loss of my first wife as my heart was overwhelmed with loneliness, hopelessness, and despair. I have also experienced His grace as God restored joy and purpose, bringing to me one of His most precious jewels—His beloved daughter, Donna.

His grace is extended to each one of us every time we repent for sinning in some way. In the beauty of a rainbow after a summer shower, we are reminded of the covenant promises we have in Christ and again His grace is made known. Over and over, He pours out on each of us this wonderful gift of grace, expressing His heart and love for us.

His grace can be expressed through friends and loved ones or through the beauty of His creation; yet we can miss it, because we have become so familiar with it that our hearts lose that childlike wonder and gratitude. At times we fail to see it because our hearts have been so captured by the cares of the world instead of the wonder of who He is to us. We fail to realize that our cares are important to Him, too. Peter reminds us to cast *"all your care upon Him, for He cares for you"* (1 Pet. 5:7).

Jesus said:

> *Assuredly, I say to you, unless you are converted and become as little children, you will by no means enter the kingdom of heaven. (Matt. 18:3)*

I believe this has a two-fold meaning: first, in order to be saved and enter the kingdom, we must come simply by faith as a child and receive His free gift of salvation through the grace of Christ; and second, in order to continue to grow in the kingdom, we must maintain that childlike wonder and trust in a Father whose love for us is eternal.

If you will allow Him, His grace will transform your heart and you will discover who you are, who He is, and who you are in Him. Allow the wonder and beauty of this gift of grace to impact you in a way that will not only change you but will touch all those around you. We were created to be world changers, to bring the will and purpose of heaven to earth in order that all might know and experience the Father's grace and be a part of His family and kingdom.

CHAPTER 11

FORGIVENESS

A Sinful Woman Forgiven

In Luke 7:36-50, we read about Simon, the Pharisee, inviting Jesus to his house to eat. A notoriously sinful woman in the city heard about it, and taking along an alabaster flask of fragrant oil, she found her way to Him. Weeping, she began to wash His feet with her tears, and wiped them with the hair of her head. She kissed His feet and anointed them with the fragrant oil. Can you imagine wiping someone's dirty feet with your hair and then kissing those feet? But this wasn't just anyone—this was *Jesus*.

The Pharisee murmured to himself, "If He were a prophet, He would know what kind of woman was touching Him—she's a sinner!"

Jesus said, *"Simon I have something to say to you."* With Simon's permission, He continued: *"There was a certain creditor who had two debtors. One owed five hundred denarii, and the other fifty. And when they had nothing with which to repay, he freely forgave them both. Tell Me, therefore, which of them will love him more?"*

Simon said he supposed the one who had been forgiven more and Jesus said, *"You have rightly judged."*

Then turning to the woman, Jesus went on: *"Do you see this woman? I entered your house; you gave Me no water for My feet, but she has washed My feet with her tears and wiped them with the hair of her head. You gave Me no kiss, but this woman has not ceased to kiss My feet since the time I came in. You did not anoint My head with oil, but this woman has anointed My feet with fragrant oil."*

Now it became obvious that the two debtors in Jesus' story represented the Pharisee and the woman. Simon, the Pharisee, had not even shown Jesus the respect that was customary for guests in that day. He had not offered water to wash the feet of Jesus or greeted Him with the customary kiss. But the woman poured out her love from a truly contrite heart. *"Therefore I say to you, her sins, which are many, are forgiven, for she loved much. But to whom little is forgiven, the same loves little."* Then He said to her, *"Your sins are forgiven."*

The people present were shocked and wondered who this man was that he could forgive sins. Then Jesus said to the woman, *"Your faith has saved you. Go in peace."*

It doesn't say that she said anything at all to Jesus. It doesn't say that she asked Him to forgive her sins; she simply laid her repentant heart at His feet. Jesus knew her heart and said that her faith had saved her. What a compassionate savior!

Oh, the wonder of the mercy and grace of our loving Heavenly Father! God had orchestrated this moment in time in order to reveal His heart and love to this woman and to set her free from the lies and wounds that had so entrapped her. She was free—free to be who He made her to be—not to be defined by rejection but to be transformed by the wonder of the love of God. The woman that had been ravaged by life was forgiven and a heart that had been imprisoned was set free. From the heart of the Father through the words of the Son came the joy of freedom, love, acceptance, and liberty.

Embraced in love, she would enter into a relationship with a loving Heavenly Father who would walk with her all the days of her life. Not only had rejection impacted this woman's life, but her responses to that rejection had led her to experience things God had never intended for her. But now she was free and forgiven; she would become all that He planned for her from the foundation of the world. Not only does God heal the wounds of rejection, but He also forgives and cleanses us of our sins as we repent and confess our sins to Him. Once that is finished, He remembers our sins no more. In fact, He only remembers our victories in Him

---

> *Jesus' blood didn't just deal with your sin, shame, and brokenness—His blood restored all things; His blood bought complete victory; His blood brought you back into right relationship as a child of God.*[15]

It isn't hard to ask God for forgiveness; it's what He wants us to do. And the Word of God says in 1 John: *If we confess our sins, He is faithful and just to forgive us our sins and to cleanse us from all unrighteousness. (1 John 1:9)*

Some may not realize that they have sins to confess. The feelings of anger, fear, resentment, or shame that they have carried since childhood may just seem to be a part of their personality. They may not like that character trait in themselves, yet not realize that they can repent for it and ask God to remove it. Maybe it has been with them so long that they think they will always have to live with it. But that is not the truth—it isn't too late!

We come to God for forgiveness for our sins. But we also need to forgive others. We cannot expect God to forgive us while we hold a grudge against someone else.

The Power of Forgiveness

Sam's Testimony
(The name is changed to protect his privacy.)

I spent many years trying to come to grips with who I was. In my twenties and early thirties, I was frustrated by the man I had become. My father was obviously key in shaping me. Now in my mid-forties with children of my own, I wear many different hats—husband, father, and mentor, to name a few. I am a responsible, hard-working man who is viewed by others as successful in his marriage and as a father. Having said this, there is always more beneath the surface of our lives than others see or perceive, and for years, I lived with deep frustration.

I was raised in a home where my father provided for me and my siblings and taught me many good life lessons and values. I was trained to go to church, be honest, respect my elders, serve others, and work hard—doing even more than is required. I was trained to be careful with money and to avoid debt; to do my work first and then play. I was taught how to take care of a car and think through the long-term consequences of my actions. I was given a solid life foundation. Looking at my brothers and me, most people would say my father did a successful job of raising his sons—which in many ways, he did. In the world's eyes, we are all successful to varying degrees.

However, most of the life lessons were taught to me wrapped in anger, shame, and criticism. My goal during my childhood was not to make dad angry. I learned to try to do things "right" and fly underneath the radar. I learned the lessons my dad taught me, but there were secondary lessons that stuck just as deeply.

I learned to walk in fear of making mistakes. I learned that my efforts were almost never good enough—therefore, I learned to become a people pleaser. I learned to become passive and avoid conflict but also that yelling at my children and being angry would accomplish my desired outcomes; if not, I'd yell louder. I learned shame as a method of child training, and I learned to doubt myself, even though I was a pretty competent person.

In my twenties and early thirties, I would have told you that I hated all of the above secondary lessons in myself but that I seemed incapable of overcoming and changing these behaviors. I was a frustrated Christian man. I could see myself doing these things but could not gain victory and confidence over them. I walked in shame and defeat.

Gladly, I'm not that man anymore. It wasn't a one-step overnight change. I changed in stages, and when I was ready, God would give me another step in my personal process of becoming whole and putting aside my anger.

For me, a first key was putting myself into mentoring relationships with older, spiritually healthy men who spoke truth into my life. Sometimes, I would not or could not believe what they told me and even fought the truth, but it was so good for me not to walk alone. It seems that each man who walked closely with me over the years was more intense, asked harder questions, and felt more passionately about me winning victory over my anger and the wounded areas of my life. I was very intentional about pursuing these relationships. Somehow I knew I needed older, godly men.

The common theme from all of these men was to not hold onto my anger, frustration, or bitterness—to forgive my father and be free. I really struggled with this.

I could verbally say I forgave my father and really agree in my head that what they were saying was right, but doing it sincerely from my heart was very challenging. As a result, I continued to struggle with anger towards my own children.

Interestingly, I have never struggled with anger toward my wife or been verbally or emotionally abusive toward her. Growing up, I watched my dad yell at my mother with verbal and emotional abuse, and I hated it. My dad was angry with us and with my mom because he could get away with it and get what he wanted by employing anger. Even as a boy, I knew I would never do that. Praise God, I also have a wife who from day one was strong enough that she would have never put up with any of it if I had. Using it toward my children, however … I hated it in myself. Why did I do it? I still don't know if I understand how I could avoid anger towards my wife but not towards my children. I wanted so badly to be free from anger.

My freedom came in my mid-thirties because I finally forgave my father, and as a result was set free from most of my anger. My mom had separated from my dad for a number of months and was contemplating divorce. My initial response was, "It's about time…. Good for her." But as I spent time with my father during this time, I saw that he was broken, and I believe it really gave me God's perspective for him for the first time, and I saw him in a different light.

This softening in me allowed me to understand some things that I think I was blind to before. You see, my father and his siblings never talked about my grandfather—ever! He died before I was born, and I have never heard more than a couple of general stories about him. He was a very mean, angry, and abusive man. My father and his siblings were abused and wounded by him. My father has said many times, "I may make a lot of mistakes, but I'm raising you children better than my father raised me." My dad thought that this applied to his marriage as well. At least he was a better husband than his father had been. My mom's decision to leave him shattered his perceptions, and I felt sorry for him.

I finally realized there was a family heritage of anger, and I wanted to be the one to break the pattern. With Christ, I had all that I needed to break it, but unforgiveness was keeping me from being free. Seeing my dad broken, I was able to forgive him and see him as a person needing God's love and forgiveness but I also began to understand that he couldn't give what he was never given. He couldn't express tenderness and love to us children because he had never received it. He really believed that the things he could give—discipline, work ethic, etc.—were enough. I was able to accept that, in general, and I forgave him of much and actually began praying for him.

It was after this that I began to see my outbursts of anger toward my children stop. I didn't get angry over stupid things. I also began to change in other ways, and my wife began noticing. She says I started becoming more of a leader and began to step up and be more confident. I stopped trying to please people as much and gained my voice.

The root of anger and unforgiveness I had been holding onto had been crippling me, and Satan knew it and tried so desperately to keep me and my brothers in that place. My father has a history of broken relationships; my brothers also have multiple divorces and broken relationships among them. Although I accepted Jesus as my Savior when I was 18 and started the renewing of my mind and life, I still had a heritage of insecure, angry, and bitter men I was tied to because I refused to walk in forgiveness. I was set free from that heritage. Praise God!

When I was in my early forties, I was at a Christian men's conference with some older men. The topic of fathering came up, and I made a comment that indicated my dad was a jerk. Nathan, who is a pastor and Christian counselor, wrote something and then gave it to one of the other men who is a close mentor of mine.

Nathan began asking me about my dad, our history, and my history of anger and unforgiveness. After a while, he said, "You still have more to deal with regarding your father. There's a word that describes what still needs to be dealt with. I want you to just ask the Holy Spirit to show you … pray and wait until you get an answer."

After about five minutes, I said, "The only word I'm getting is contempt." Nathan asked the other man for the paper he had given him and handed it to me. On the piece of paper was written contempt. Nathan then explained that contempt is cold anger. Contempt is under the surface. It will show itself in dry comments like, "He's a jerk." It's not hot anger but buried, hidden anger.

He told me that the anger I had dealt with years earlier was that hot anger towards my dad at the really overt things. Now it was time to deal with the rest of it, even the things about him that just annoyed me, agitated me, or caused me to shake my head and walk away saying, "What a jerk." Until I could do this, I could not really love him the way Christ wanted me to, and I would not be completely free.

Conviction came over me regarding these attitudes towards my father; I asked forgiveness from God for my contempt, and I asked to be set free. That was four years ago. I can honestly say that I have not struggled with anger since then. It took forty-three years. Wow, I'm thankful. I don't want to ever carry unforgiveness in me again. It's way too heavy and exacts much too high of a price.

Parable of the Unforgiving Servant

God places high importance on forgiveness. He gave His only begotten Son, Jesus, to provide a way of forgiveness for a world of lost sinners. He expects us to extend that forgiveness to others as well. Consider the Parable of the Unforgiving Servant that Jesus shares in Matthew 18. Peter has come to Jesus and asked how many times he should forgive his brother when he sins against him— should he forgive seven times? But Jesus tells him not seven times, but up to seventy times seven times! He really isn't offering Peter a mathematical equation here. He isn't telling Peter to keep a tally and after 490 times, he doesn't have to forgive anymore, but rather He is telling him to forgive without limit.

> *"Therefore the kingdom of heaven is like a certain king who wanted to settle accounts with his servants. And when he had begun to settle accounts, one was brought to him who owed him ten thousand talents. But as he was not able to pay, his master commanded that he be sold, with his wife and children and all that he had, and that payment be made. The servant therefore fell down before him, saying, 'Master, have patience with me, and I will pay you all.' Then the master of that servant was moved with compassion, released him, and forgave him the debt. But that servant went out and found one of his fellow servants who owed him a hundred denarii; and he laid hands on him and took him by the throat, saying, 'Pay me what you owe!'*

"So his fellow servant fell down at his feet and begged him, saying, 'Have patience with me, and I will pay you all.' And he would not, but went and threw him into prison till he should pay the debt.

So when his fellow servants saw what had been done, they were very grieved, and came and told their master all that had been done. Then his master, after he had called him, said to him, 'You wicked servant! I forgave you all that debt because you begged me. Should you not also have had compassion on your fellow servant, just as I had pity on you?' And his master was angry, and delivered him to the torturers until he should pay all that was due to him. So My Heavenly Father also will do to you if each of you, from his heart, does not forgive his brother his trespasses." (Matt. 18:23-35)

Is something hindering your heart from having a close relationship with your Heavenly Father? Whether it is anger, wounds, lies, fatherlessness, shame, or fear; whatever has taken hold of your heart, ask the Holy Spirit to reveal to you what has caused these things. Maybe, like Sam, there is a need for forgiveness for someone in your life; if that is revealed, take care of it. Forgiveness is not an option. To hold unforgiveness against someone will inhibit your growth in Christ and your walk with the Lord. If we don't forgive, we create an opportunity or give place to the enemy to capture our hearts and keep us imprisoned. Don't let anger fester in your heart.

"Be angry, and do not sin": do not let the sun go down on your wrath, nor give place to the devil. (Eph. 4:26)

Romans 2:4 tells us that the kindness of God leads us to repentance. Not only must we forgive, but we must repent of holding contempt towards those who have hurt and wounded us. As God has shown me things from my own life where I was wounded, I not only have had to forgive but I have had to repent for the contempt that I had held in my heart these many years.

God shows us these things so that we might be set free from the impact of the wounds in our lives. He is a merciful God—not leaving us in our sins but showing us in His Word how to be set free of the chains that bind our hearts.

CHAPTER 12

GOD'S LOVE MANIFESTED

Throngs of people followed Jesus, listening to His teachings and asking questions. His touch brought healing and many were set free from things that had held them captive for many years. The Jewish leaders felt threatened by the way the people loved Jesus and were attempting to catch Him in some error or call into question His credibility. Jesus didn't let their questions interfere with His teachings but instead utilized them to teach more important life lessons.

A Lawyer Asks How to Inherit Eternal Life

A lawyer once tested Jesus by asking Him what he needed to do to inherit eternal life. Turning the question back to him, Jesus asked what he had read in the Law.

"'You shall love the Lord your God with all your heart, with all your soul, with all your strength, and with all your mind,' and 'your neighbor as yourself,'" the lawyer replied

And Jesus said to him, "You have answered rightly; do this and you will live."

Not yet ready to give up, the lawyer pressed on. "'And who is my neighbor?'" he asked, in an effort to justify himself.

The Good Samaritan

Then Jesus answered and said: "A certain man went down from Jerusalem to Jericho, and fell among thieves, who stripped him of his clothing, wounded him, and departed, leaving him half dead. Now by chance a certain priest came down that road. And when he saw him, he passed by on the other side. Likewise a Levite, when he arrived at the place, came and looked, and passed by on the other side. But a certain Samaritan, as he journeyed, came where he was. And when he saw him, he had compassion. So he went to him and bandaged his wounds, pouring on oil and wine; and he set him on his own animal, brought him to an inn, and took care of him. On the next day, when he departed, he took out two denarii, gave them to the innkeeper, and said to him, 'Take care of him; and whatever more you spend, when I come again, I will repay you.' So which of these three do you think was neighbor to him who fell among the thieves?"

And he said, "He who showed mercy on him."

Then Jesus said to him, "Go and do likewise."(Luke 10:30-37)

Jesus could have chosen anyone for the character of the good neighbor in His parable, but He chose a Samaritan. He used the least likely person—from the Jewish perspective—to be the good neighbor in His story. In doing so, He revealed the Father's own character, demonstrating it through the life of this Samaritan man; He depicted what the love of God actually looks like.

We can draw numerous observations from this story. The most important is how God really views each one of us. Keep in mind that the Jews hated the Samaritans at that time, considering them a mixed breed that used many pagan practices in their worship. Yet through this Samaritan character, Jesus demonstrates the Father's love—even for those whom society considers the least.

The opinions of man do not influence God. The Apostle John shared in his letters, *"We love Him because*

> *The love of God is uninfluenced.*
> *God is free, spontaneous, uncaused.*[16]

He first loved us" (1 John 4:19). His love isn't based on my love for Him but on His love for me. Being the very origin of love, His love for me is not based on anything I have done but purely on whom He is—no one could ever do enough to earn His love. Paul writes in his letters to the Romans:

> *But God demonstrates His own love toward us, in that while we were still sinners, Christ died for us. (Rom. 5:8)*

I know what I was like before Christ, and yet He loved me and He still loves me. His love is eternal, indisputable, and never changing; it is infinite, holy, and gracious. It isn't dependent on anything we have done or haven't done but on who He is—for God is love. The enemy would have us believe otherwise, using lies in an attempt to turn our eyes from the truth of the immutability of God.

ॐॐॐॐ

Karen's Testimony
(The name has been changed to protect her privacy.)

It took many years and intentional work to undo and forgive many things and people from my childhood that had caused a wounding and brokenness in my life. Those things didn't happen overnight. But with the help and guidance of the Holy Spirit, I was able to forgive and re-place the lies and hurts with the truths and love that my Heavenly Father had intended for me to experience all along. He showed me what it was like to be truly fathered, truly unconditionally loved by a father; loved simply be-cause I was His daughter; loved because of who He made me and who He knew I would become because He make all things good.

Leaving condemnation and accusation behind, I now walk a path of discovery and adventure. Discovering all that is available to me because I am a daughter of the King of Kings! I truly am a princess; I have a great inheritance, not because of any merits of my own but because of who He is! Now life is an adventure, I have a purpose; I expect great things ahead because He walks with me and is in me. Nothing is impossible in your life when the creator of the universe is your Daddy!

The Holy Spirit wants to reveal the truth about God's great love, exposing the lies of the enemy, healing the broken-hearted, and setting the captive free.

> *Then Jesus said to those Jews who believed Him, "If you abide in My word, you are My disciples indeed. And you shall know the truth, and the truth shall make you free." Therefore if the Son makes you free, you shall be free indeed. (John 8:31)*

Zacchaeus

We mentioned previously that tax collectors in Jesus' day were in many ways outcasts in society. They could actually walk up to an individual and tax him for what he was carrying, and much more. The fact that they were usually fellow-Jews, who worked for Rome, made them all the more despised. Zacchaeus was a chief tax collector and very rich. Although his name meant "clean" or "pure," his life did not reflect that purity.

It started out like any other day in Jericho; Zacchaeus was busy carrying out his typical duties as a tax collector. However, this day would be unlike any other day in his life. Today he would be encountered by the Creator of the entire universe—*his* Creator! While walking down the streets of Jericho, he heard a great commotion. What could possibly be going on? Being very short in stature, Zacchaeus was unable to see over the crowd, so he began to inquire of those around him. Some of the crowd told him that it was Jesus, the One who had done incredible miracles; Jesus was coming their way.

Zacchaeus had heard stories about Jesus but had never actually seen Him. He quickly climbed a tree in order to see Jesus over the crowd. Can you imagine this well-known businessman scrambling up a tree like a curious little school boy?

This is what our journey is all about—seeing Him; and in seeing Him, we discover who He really is and who we truly are. Like Zacchaeus, the ravages of this world have so injured many of us in one way or another that we live our lives behind a false pretense. This façade is a defense mechanism we have created in order to cover up our inner agony and struggles. You can be sure that Zacchaeus suffered from cruel remarks about his stature as well as from the shame in his heart for the way he had used his position in order to gain riches. But today God would encounter him in such a profound way that he would never be the same. Using our creative imaginations, we can see the heart of God unfold before us in this story.

> Then Jesus entered and passed through Jericho. Now behold, there was a man named Zacchaeus who was a chief tax collector, and he was rich. And he sought to see who Jesus was, but could not because of the crowd, for he was of short stature. So he ran ahead and climbed up into a sycamore tree to see Him, for He was going to pass that way. And when Jesus came to the place, He looked up and saw him, and said to him, "Zacchaeus, make haste and come down, for today I must stay at your house."

So he made haste and came down, and received Him joyfully. But when they saw it, they all complained, saying, "He has gone to be a guest with a man who is a sinner."

Then Zacchaeus stood and said to the Lord, "Look, Lord, I give half of my goods to the poor; and if I have taken anything from anyone by false accusation, I restore fourfold."

And Jesus said to him, "Today salvation has come to this house, because he also is a son of Abraham; for the Son of Man has come to seek and to save that which was lost." (Luke 19:1-10)

We can imagine how stunned Zacchaeus must have been when Jesus stood beneath the sycamore tree and told him to hurry down because He was going to his house. Overwhelmed with joy, Zacchaeus scurried down the tree to meet Jesus. This Man who had taught about the kingdom of God and had done incredible miracles wanted to have fellowship with him in his home!

Those standing nearby couldn't believe what they had just heard and began to grumble because Jesus was going to be Zacchaeus' guest. Of all of the good people in this crowd, why would Jesus choose to associate with this sinner?

Surely no expense was spared in the feast prepared at Zacchaeus's home for his honored guest. Then, as they were dining, Zacchaeus suddenly stood and made this surprising statement, *"Look, Lord, I give half of my goods to the poor; and if I have taken anything from anyone by false accusation, I restore fourfold."* He was giving up a lot and it was in stark contrast to the way he had lived his life up to that time. Zacchaeus had very likely experienced much unkindness and rejection in his life as a result of being so short. Possibly, the rejection and deep pain in his heart had caused him to make a vow that no matter the cost, he would make something of himself. The profession that he had chosen would not only make him wealthy, but respected (though not loved), because he represented Rome. The power that he wielded over those in his society gave him a sense of increased stature, and he had become highly successful. What could have brought Zacchaeus to declare this amazing turn-around?

God's Lovingkindness

Like each of us, Zacchaeus longed to be loved and accepted. He was ashamed of what he had become. Enjoying a delicious meal and wonderful fellowship with Jesus, Zacchaeus' heart began to soften. This Man, Jesus, knew everything about him, yet had never once judged or condemned him—in fact, He had offered acceptance and love. The lovingkindness of Jesus had won his heart. In that moment, he discovered who he was and what he had been created to be. The same One who dined with him that day realized his pain and had come that day to heal and set him free. No longer would he be an outcast of society and an orphan; now he would be a beloved son of God forever.

Jesus had sought him out and brought salvation to his lost soul. What Zacchaeus experienced that day was the grace and mercy of the Father that flowed out of His eternal lovingkindness. Not only did he experience the eternal lovingkindness of the Father, but also the mercy and grace of God through forgiveness; he was called into his true identity—Zacchaeus: the pure, clean, beloved son of God.

Like Zacchaeus, we live our lives caught up in the sin of this world. We are lost children, orphans, and strangers trying to find our way in a world where we don't belong. There is nothing lovable about us in our sinful state and nothing that we can do would ever earn that kind of love. But Christ—the Messiah, the Anointed One—died for us while we were still sinners and paid the price for us to be called the children of God.

> But God demonstrates His own love toward us, in that while we were still sinners, Christ died for us. (Rom. 5:8)

Abby's Testimony

Abby Johnson, author of *Unplanned*, was a young university student who was recruited by Planned Parenthood. She quickly advanced to the position of director of one of the largest abortion providers in the state of Texas. Abby originally joined this nonprofit organization because of a strong desire to truly help women in need in a time of crisis. After eight years with the organization, the truth of what was behind the corporation became increasingly clear—they were selling the product *abortion* for profit.

What is truly amazing about her journey is that as the Lord was drawing her out of the entanglement of Planned Parenthood, she ended up running to the very group that had walked and prayed and demonstrated love to her for years outside on Planned Parenthood's sidewalk. Over the years, the Coalition for Life had demonstrated the love of Christ personally to Abby and to the clients of Planned Parenthood. It was His love expressed through them to her that caused her eyes to be opened to see the truth of the service her employer provider. On the day she left her career with Planned Parenthood, she instinctively knew that her "opposition" was a safe place to run to because day by day they had demonstrated the love of God as they silently prayed outside her facility. Abby saw and felt the true Gospel of "love your enemies" impacting her in a powerful and dramatic way.

Today Abby is actively involved in the Pro-Life movement and is now not only serving women in crisis but saving the lives of the preborn. Because the pro-lifers were not condemning her, judging her, and venting anger at her, Abby could instead see and hear the love and feel the power of their loving prayers; that was the "good news" that was used to open her heart and lead her from a life of death into the journey of eternal life in Christ and a relationship with the Father.

God's Love Heals the Brokenhearted

> *But those things which proceed out of the mouth come from the heart, and they defile a man. For out of the heart proceed evil thoughts, murders, adulteries, fornications, thefts, false witness, blasphemies. (Matt. 15:18-19)*

Toxic words, thoughts, and deeds—all kinds of damage can issue from the broken-hearted. Twisted thoughts and emotions, spite, distrust, longings, envy, and deceitfulness as well as desperate searching for physical comforts in the form of addictions, sexual gratifications, and overeating; all result from a broken heart. Life is viewed from a position of pain—made profane and defiled. But God heals broken hearts. He is filled and overflowing with love, grace, and healing. If your heart has been broken, there is only One who can put the pieces back together and make your heart into that beautiful masterpiece that God intended for it to be.

Saved by Love

The Apostle John's letters were filled with words like: "Perfect love casts out all fear…" (1 John 4:18), "God is love" (1 John 4:8), and "let us not love in word or tongue, but in action and truth" (1 John 3:18). And he says "What manner of love the Father has bestowed on us, that we should be called children of God" (1 John 3:1).

In this the love of God was manifested toward us, that God has sent His only begotten Son into the world, that we might live through Him. In this is love, not that we loved God, but that He loved us and sent His Son to be the propitiation for our sins. Beloved, if God so loved us, we also ought to love one another. (1 John 4:9-11)

The Father has all of the answers that we are seeking. He made the way easy—He gave us Jesus.

CHAPTER 13

TRUSTING IN THE FATHER

Trust

You will trust God only as much as you love Him. And you will love Him not because you have studied Him; you will love Him because you have touched Him in response to His touch. Only if you love, will you make that final leap into darkness. "Father into your hands I commend my spirit."[17]

What a tremendous quote! This quote reminds me of the innocent child leaping through the air into the extended arms of someone that he trusts. That trusted person will not drop their arms or let them fall. This is the essence of our journey into the Father's heart—to know Him and love Him so much that we will trust Him enough to leap blindly into His outstretched arms knowing He will *never* let us down; He will *never* fail us. On this journey, we are discovering more and more about who our Heavenly Father really is. We are learning to love Him and trust Him more because of who He is and because of who we are in Him.

While attending a father/son retreat, the Lord spoke to me about a particular Scripture that He had placed in my heart some 37 years ago when I first became a Christian.

Trust in the Lord with all your heart, And lean not on your own understanding; In all your ways acknowledge Him, And He shall direct your paths. (Prov. 3:5-6)

These verses have been a wonderful compass in my life, and I have read and quoted them numerous times over the years. When I have entered places in my life where the road ahead wasn't clear, I would take refuge in these words. And so, while I was on this retreat, God made it clear that He wanted me to study and meditate upon one word out of these verses—the word *trust*.

Looking at the meaning of trust in the context of this passage, I learned several things. Trust means "to be dependent upon, hope in, and rely upon." It means "to have confidence in; be confident." It means "to be bold, be secure, or make secure." And it means "to feel safe; be careless."

Pondering these meanings, I realized that I wasn't fully trusting God in every area of my life. Several meanings that stood out for me were, "to be secure, to feel safe," and "to be careless." For many of us, trust has been a major issue throughout our lives. It has influenced our most intimate relationships and the way we live our lives, as well as affecting the way we respond to others and to God.

If we let these two small verses become a way of life, they will change how we see God and ourselves. In so doing, it will transform us from the inside out and bring us into the liberty of the children of God.

Don't rush past the word *trust* without allowing the Holy Spirit to speak to you concerning areas of your life where you have held mistrust toward others and more importantly, toward God. Doing so will prevent you from experiencing the freedom that the Father desires for you.

At times Jesus said things that mystified His listeners. On one such occasion, Jesus shared, *"unless you eat the flesh of the Son of Man and drink His blood, you have no life in you" (John 6:53).* It was a very hard word to comprehend, and as a result, many left. They didn't understand, so they didn't trust Him. As they left, Jesus turned to His disciples and said, *"Do you also want to go away?"*

To this Peter replied, *"Lord, to whom shall we go? You have the words of eternal life."* Peter was saying, "I have been with you long enough to trust you even when I don't understand what you say."

Years ago, my family and I were on a flight to England. As we approached the airport, I noticed that the sky below us was totally overcast. Beginning to descend, the aircraft entered into the clouds. I heard the engines and felt the movement of the plane, but I had no idea where we were. Because of the severely overcast skies, I assumed that there were numerous aircraft arriving at the same time and that the control tower was separating them so each could land safely. I thought that our pilots must have been instructed to hold their position until it was our turn to land. I remember thinking we must be quite high and there certainly must be a large number of aircraft waiting so it would be some time until we landed. Still lost in my thoughts, I heard the familiar sound of the tires touching the runway. I was stunned.

Looking out the window, I couldn't see a thing; nor could the pilots. However, numerous sophisticated instruments in the cockpit guided them into a proper approach, showing them what their altitude was, the rate of decline, and their approach speed. A "heads up" screen showed them a glide path upon which to fly in order to land safely. Having flown hundreds of hours through all types of weather, the pilots had become very familiar with these instruments, and as a result, they trusted with absolute confidence that the instruments were correct. Although they had entered into a dense fog, they landed safely because they trusted the instruments that were guiding them.

God's Word is like the instruments pilots use, and it will guide us every day of our lives if we let it—but just how effective it is in our lives depends on us. Like the pilots, we must trust God and His Word. Even though we cannot see what lies ahead, we can trust His Word to direct us and keep us on the narrow pathway that leads to eternal life. A powerful revelation in Psalm 138:2 says, *"...You have magnified Your word above all Your name."* And in Numbers 23:19, it says, *"God is not a man that He should lie,"* so when God declares a thing, He stands by it. You can trust His Word for it will never change. As the pilots trust their flight instruments to direct their flight patterns, so we can trust the Word of God to direct our life patterns— and even more so, because God can *never fail*; He will not let us down.

One definition of trust is, "assured reliance on the character, ability, strength, or truth of someone or something." For some, to have trust in anyone or anything has been a challenge. Their distrust may have resulted from being abandoned by a parent or parents at a young age. In turn, this wounding created in their heart a sense of insecurity and lack of trust that has followed them all of their lives. It has influenced their relationships, decisions, thoughts, and actions preventing them from trusting anyone—including God.

If they never get past this point in their lives, they will continue to lean on their own understanding thus prohibiting them from acknowledging God and entering into an intimate relationship with Him, which may in turn cause them to stray from Him, from their destiny, purpose, and from all those they love. However, being the good Father that He is, God will continue to pursue them with love.

Distrust plays havoc in relationships. For many this lack of trust in others twists itself around to become a feeling that others distrust *them*—which then becomes rejection. This carries over to their relationship with God since they are not able to fully trust Him either. As they allow more and more rejection (real or imagined) into their lives, they draw farther and farther away from a deep personal relationship with the Father.

The Parable of the Lost Sheep

"See that you do not look down on one of these little ones. For I tell you that their angels in heaven always see the face of my Father in heaven. What do you think? If a man owns a hundred sheep, and one of them wanders away, will he not leave the ninety-nine on the hills and go to look for the one that wandered off? And if he finds it, I tell you the truth, he is happier about that one sheep than about the ninety-nine that did not wander off. In the same way your Father in heaven is not willing that any of these little ones should be lost." (Matt. 18:10-14)

This parable is very similar to the one in Luke 15 where Jesus was speaking to the Pharisees, scribes, sinners, and tax collectors. Each time He revisits this parable, Jesus is revealing the heart of the Father for every broken, lost soul that has strayed from God's original plan and purpose for their lives in order to pursue their own plan. But that is not what He wants. He wants them to return to Him, and He continues to pursue them in His great love and mercy.

The Lord is not slack concerning His promise as some count slackness, but is longsuffering toward us, not willing that any should perish but that all should come to repentance." (2 Pet. 3:9)

In Proverbs 14, we find:

There is a way that seems right to a man, but its end is the way of death. (Prov. 14:12)

This is true of those who haven't received Christ as their Lord and Savior as well as for those who have. Man's own ways lead to fruitlessness or to eternal death.

Through the parable of the lost sheep, Jesus reveals the Father as the Good Shepherd, who has pursued us all of our lives. His pursuit has been for the sole purpose of restoring our relationship with Him and for restoring the plans and purposes He has destined for each one of us. By His Holy Spirit, the Father revealed the truth of the Gospel of Christ and of the great sacrifice He made in order to restore us to His original design. As we heard (not just with our ears but with our hearts), by faith we have received Jesus Christ as our Lord and Savior. And in that moment that we received Jesus, the Father did something amazing. He adopted us and made us into sons and daughters of the Most High God.

Who hath delivered us from the power of darkness, and hath translated us into the kingdom of His dear Son. (Col. 1:13 KJV)

Rejection

Legally, we are no longer under the influence of the evil one. The Scriptures tell us we are free. But for many, like me, when we first got saved, we were not able to accept the full love of the Father. We still responded to God like an orphan would. But why was that? I believe it was because we had allowed the enemy to use one of his most insidious weapons—rejection. This he used with the premeditated purpose of leading us astray from this glorious fellowship with the Father.

Whether experienced from your family, close friends, or someone else, rejection can impact your heart in a way that restrains your relationship with the Father. Rejection is in opposition to acceptance. In many cases, both the church and the world have expressed their acceptance or rejection of us based on our performance.

On the other hand, the Father expresses His love through His grace, mercy, and truth which He fully revealed through the Cross. These are the characteristics of the Father that Jesus is communicating through the parable of the lost sheep—both for the lost sinner and for those who have been led astray through rejection. Rejection leads us to believe that we can't trust anyone—not even God.

৵৵৵৵

Todd's Testimony

Todd, the youngest of three brothers, grew up in northeast Nebraska in a small town of 8000. At the age of five, he and his family moved to Wyoming where his father managed oil fields. During this time his father had his first nervous breakdown resulting in his being institutionalized. He suffered two more breakdowns, one when Todd was eight and again when he was ten.

I asked Todd how this had impacted him as a young child. He remembers saying, "Be careful, you don't know when life will blow up." He shouldn't have had a care in the world at such a young age, but the traumatic events that he faced brought with them this feeling of insecurity and impending danger. These events created fear and mistrust, and the enemy used them to capture and shape

Todd's heart, leading him astray from God's purpose and destiny for him.

Todd remembers his dad as a man who "never had time for me" and was incapable of expressing love. He had a fierce temper. One day when he was just six years old, Todd watched his father break a pool cue over his eleven-year-old brother. You can imagine the lasting impression that left in his young heart. Although his father was highly regarded by others, Todd never trusted him and held deep bitterness toward him.

His mother spent her time and energy in an attempt to make his father happy, thus she had little or no time for Todd. Because his mom worked outside of the home and his father traveled often, Todd became what is known as a latchkey kid.

When he was fifteen, Todd's mother purchased a small farm for his dad where he could keep his horses. It was in order to keep him happy, but soon afterwards, his father suffered a severe heart attack, dying moments before his mother arrived at the hospital.

"Soon afterwards my elder brother and his new wife came to live with us....Dad died in December, and in April I found my mom hanging from the garage rafters."

I can't begin to imagine how traumatic these events must have been for him. Not only had he suffered rejection by his father, but now he was abandoned by his mother as well.

Todd became a Christian, active in Young Life during high school and eventually became a youth pastor. Still he continually viewed God as distant and not living inside of him. "I was emotionally mixed up and unable to keep my life together." It finally surfaced when his future wife confronted him that he was codependent and controlling.

Although Todd received some healing through

professional counseling, the real healing came when he was invited by Richard Dungan to participate in a men's retreat. I have personally seen Richard father many sons. He has a unique ability to create a safe environment in which orphans can come to the realization that they are truly sons. He has been able to do so because he himself was a spiritual orphan. During this time away in a safe environment, Todd felt free enough to unpack all the pain and hurt that he had suffered.

Todd's greatest desire was to have a father who would have time for him, dream with him, help him, and lead him in a safe and secure relationship. He was able to find this kind of relationship as Richard mentored him, and as Todd was able to trust, it helped him embark on this incredible journey into the Father's heart. Today Todd knows who he is, what his purpose is in life, where he is going, and who His Heavenly Father truly is. Today he can say, "I am no longer an orphan."

Todd has discovered the joys of knowing the Father in a growing, intimate relationship. As a result, he is able to lead those who have, like himself, been led astray by the pains and wounds of life.

Years ago Todd found that he was unable to dream because as a child he had observed that when his dad dreamed he would ultimately have a nervous breakdown. The enemy created fear in Todd's heart as he spoke to him the lie that if you ever attempt to dream, you will suffer a nervous breakdown too. Now, because he understands that he is a beloved son of the Father—not just in his mind but in his heart as well—he can actually dream.

In his final comments, Todd said, "I understand who I am and now I can help others meet the Father. That is when I feel most alive."

ॐॐॐॐ

Todd's testimony is one about a loving, caring Heavenly Father who continued to pursue him when the lies and wounds of the enemy had led him astray. Like the shepherd went after the lost lamb and returned him to the fold, the Father pursued Todd and brought him into the kingdom of His dear Son.

Within each of us, there is a deep hunger to be loved and accepted. We long to discover the answers to who we are, where we are going, what our purpose is, what our destiny is, who God is, and how He sees and relates to us. When painful things happen in our lives, especially at a young and vulnerable age, our souls become wounded, our hearts become broken, our dreams are crushed, and our desires remain unfulfilled. We see life and ourselves through clouded lenses, believing the lies of the enemy that there is no one that we can trust—not even God. I am convinced that many live their lives today with hidden, intense suffering because they are unable to make any sense out of the way life has so wounded them.

Many, like Todd, have found themselves on a journey to discover answers to those questions. In order to create a safe environment where they won't be hurt again, people construct a false persona behind which they hide in order to receive love and acceptance. Their deepest pains and wounds remain locked away in the hidden recesses of their hearts, and their deception carries over from themselves to those they love.

The Father is the Master Shepherd. His true nature is reflected in the lives of those who have allowed Him to walk with them, healing the pains and wounds of their lives. The true nature of our Heavenly Father is revealed in the story of the stray sheep. The Father deploys all the resources of heaven to restore and redeem one stray lamb—one stray child of God. Our Father is trustworthy, loving, kind, compassionate, eternally faithful, and good.

The Father will come and walk with you if you will just ask Him to. Let Him reach down into the deepest recesses of your heart, taking away the pain, healing the wounds, setting you free, and bringing you into the light of His love. You can trust Him—He is safe. You will also be able to say, *"I am no longer an orphan—I am His beloved son."*

Acceptance For Rejection

Allowing the world to define your identity will lead to shipwreck. Your identity is defined by who you are in Him; you are His beloved sons and daughters. God's labor on the Cross stands as undeniable proof that we are loved and accepted.

Rejection is one of the cruelest weapons of the enemy. He deploys it through others for the sole purpose of diminishing or destroying our relationship with the Father and the destiny and potential that God has for each of us.

Years ago I was traveling in Asia with a ministry team that was serving missionaries on the field. One of the team members there was a trained counselor, and he was doing some personal one-on-one counseling. He invited me to sit in on the sessions and pray for him and the individuals as they spent time together. As I prayed quietly, I was able to hear what was being said. The counselor asked a man this question, "What was your childhood like?"

The man thought for a moment and then responded, "I never really had a childhood."

Can you explain?" asked the counselor. "Well you see I was raised in a very strict home and I was never allowed to be a child." I thought how incredible that sounded and wondered what he meant. The counselor asked him to explain further, so he continued. "You see, my parents always treated me as an adult and not as a child and expected me to act like an adult as well, not a child." When the counselor asked if he had liked that, he replied, "No, I did not."

"Well, from the depths of your heart, how did you really feel about them?" the counselor inquired.

This man had been serving as a missionary of the Gospel for over 25 years in this country; yet, he had suffered from rejection since he was a child. As I listened, the missionary thought for a moment and then he looked at the counselor with almost rage in his eyes and said, "I hated them; they stole my childhood!"

I was stunned. I couldn't believe what I was hearing, and then the Holy Spirit spoke to me at almost the same moment, "And you had your childhood stolen as well." It shook me to the very core of my being; yet, it was true. Like this man, I had been deeply wounded by rejection, also—not in the exact same way, but still rejected. All human beings desire to be accepted for who they are.

Mercy Ship

Recently my wife and I watched a documentary about a Mercy Ship that had been working in an African country for many months. Much of what they did involved surgery on patients who suffered horrible defects from benign tumors. These tumors erupted on the faces of the individuals, causing them to look like they had been made up for a movie. One lady had an immense growth protruding out of her chin. Because of the hideous deformity, she had been rejected by her husband. Others were so deformed by these tumors that they only had one good eye. There were so many suffering with this horrible malady.

The mission of this Mercy Ship was twofold. Of course, the surgical removal of the tumors and repairing the damage was major, but to me, the second thing was more important. Their intended purpose was to bring hope to each one of these individuals, saying through their actions, "You are loved and accepted just the way you are."

The host of this documentary interviewed one of the nurses who had served on the ship for over four years. He asked her this question, "Are you not put off by their deformities?"

"At first I was, until I realized that there was a person, a human being in there, one who needed to be recognized." She had seen the heart of the one who hungered to be accepted.

Maybe you don't have an outward tumor but instead one has grown in your heart. It implanted itself there and began to grow the day you were rejected by those who were meant to love and nurture you. It has created within your heart fear, confusion, anger, and low self-esteem. As a result, it caused you to create a *false* self, which is a tumor that prevents you from becoming who you were created to be. If you let Him, the Great Physician will remove this hideous wound, replacing it with Himself, and give you a new identity.

CHAPTER 14

THE CROSS—GOD'S RESCUE PLAN

Called to Be a King

As a young boy, David spent much of his time alone in the wilderness pastures of Palestine, tending his father's sheep. During those times out in the beauty of nature, David discovered the Father and who he was in Him. These times prepared him for the day when God would anoint him as king of Israel.

One day God called Samuel, His prophet, saying,

"Fill your horn with oil, and go; I am sending you to Jesse the Bethlehemite. For I have provided Myself a king among his sons."(1 Sam. 16:1)

God told Samuel to take a heifer and invite Jesse along to sacrifice it. So he went and consecrated Jesse and his sons and invited them to the sacrifice. Then Samuel asked Jesse to have each one of his sons pass before him in order for the Lord to select one to be king. Jesse saw no reason to call his youngest son in from the field where he was minding the sheep, but he had each of his seven other sons pass before Samuel, one by one. God, the Lord, rejected each one.

And the Lord said to Samuel,

…the Lord does not see as man sees; for man looks at the outward appearance, but the Lord looks at the heart. (1 Sam. 16:7)

This is such a key point for you to see concerning your-self. Your father and mother may have rejected and dis-qualified you—but your Heavenly Father has not. In fact, Psalms says:

When my father and my mother forsake me, then the Lord will take care of me. (Psalms 27:10)

"The Lord has not chosen these" (1 Sam. 16:10) Samuel said to Jesse, and asked him if there were any more young men. Jesse told him that the youngest was keeping the sheep. Then David was sent for, and as he came before Samuel, the Lord said, *"Arise, anoint him; for this is the one!" (1 Sam. 16:12).*

When Samuel came, for whatever reason, David was excluded from joining his father and brothers but he was not disqualified in the eyes of the Father. David's family may not have respected him; yet, his name meant be-loved or loved one and reflected the heart of the Father towards him—he was fully qualified and accepted by the Father to such an extent that he was chosen above all of the rest of his brothers to be king of Israel.

Samuel had told Saul earlier:

But now your kingdom shall not continue. The Lord has sought for Himself a man after His own heart, and the Lord has commanded him to be commander over His people, because you have not kept what the Lord commanded you. (1 Sam. 13:14)

The man after God's own heart was David, al-though Samuel did not know that yet. It was after this pronouncement that God sent Samuel to anoint one of Jesse's sons and David was called forth for that appointment.

Jesus Cleanses the Leper

The lepers were another example of someone that was looked down upon. Back in Jesus' day, leprosy was an incurable disease, and lepers were isolated from the rest of society and even shunned by their own families. They were not allowed to go home until they were officially recognized as clean. As a Jew, the one who was infected would have to come before the priest and undergo certain prescribed things in order to be acknowledged as clean. Anyone who had contact with them was also considered to be unclean, but in this encounter, we find Jesus compassionately reaching out to touch the leper who knelt before Him begging for His healing touch.

> *Now a leper came to Him, imploring Him, kneeling down to Him and saying to Him, "If You are willing, You can make me clean." Then Jesus, moved with compassion, stretched out His hand and touched him, and said to him, "I am willing; be cleansed." (Mark 1:40-41)*

Can you imagine how Jesus must have felt? This poor man was desperate to be healed! I know the emotions I feel when someone in my family is in pain, and I am sure they are similar to what Jesus must have felt. It says here that Jesus was moved with compassion. He does what He sees His Father doing; He reached out His hand and touched the leper saying *"I am willing; be cleansed,"* and immediately the leper was made whole.

Blind Bartimaeus

Continuing our journey on through Jericho, we discover a blind man by the name of Bartimaeus.

> *Then they came to Jericho. As Jesus and His disciples, together with a large crowd, were leaving the city, a blind*

man, Bartimaeus (that is, the Son of Timaeus), was sitting by the roadside begging. When he heard that it was Jesus of Nazareth, he began to shout, "Jesus, Son of David, have mercy on me!" Many rebuked him and told him to be quiet, but he shouted all the more, "Son of David, have mercy on me!" Jesus stopped and said, "Call him." So they called to the blind man, "Cheer up! On your feet! He's calling you." Throwing his cloak aside, he jumped to his feet and came to Jesus. "What do you want me to do for you?" Jesus asked him. The blind man said, "Rabbi, I want to see." "Go," said Jesus, "your faith has healed you." Immediately he received his sight and followed Jesus along the road. (Mark 10:46-52)

Jesus was passing through Jericho, heading toward Jerusalem and the Cross. There is no account of Him touching or healing anyone in Jericho. But on the outskirts of town was a beggar by the name of Bartimaeus. Born blind, he had suffered years of isolation and abuse by those who passed by. Daily he would wait along the dusty road that led out of the city, begging because that was all he knew to do. Can you imagine what despair he must have felt? Do you suppose he ever felt accepted and loved?

Bartimaeus had lived in a world of total darkness without hope of it ever being otherwise until he heard about the man people called the Son of David or Jesus, who was healing the sick and performing many awesome miracles throughout the land. In his heart, it sparked a hope that perhaps he might one day meet Jesus too. Maybe He would heal him and give him the sight that he so longed for. As Jesus approached him, He heard Bartimaeus' cry and then, following the Father's direction, Jesus healed him.

To the local people, Bartimaeus was just a blind beggar who would never be otherwise, the son of Timaeus; someone to be despised or perhaps pitied. But the Father had known Bartimaeus and loved him from all eternity. *"Son of David, have mercy on me!"* Bartimaeus shouted. People around him told him to be quiet, but he only yelled louder, determined to do whatever was in his power to get through to Jesus—He was his only hope. Then the people told him that Jesus was calling to him. Overwhelmed with anticipation, blind Bartimaeus threw aside his garment of shame, brokenness, and lies of the enemy and got up and came before Jesus.

How many of us have worn this same garment? This familiar garment has blinded us to the wonder, the beauty, and the true nature and character of our Father.

Kneeling before Jesus, Bartimaeus heard these words, *"What do you want Me to do for you?"*

Bartimaeus responded, *"Rabbi, I want to see."*

The answer seems so obvious that we sometimes wonder why Jesus even asked him that question—surely He already knew; yet, Jesus is asking you and me that same question, "What do you want Me to do for you?"

Our response may be much like this, "I want to see—to see who You truly are and who You made me to be. I want to see what my purpose and destiny is. I have been blinded for so long by the wounds and lies of the enemy and now You have come my way, sent by my Heavenly Father, and I want to receive my sight."

Jesus told Bartimaeus, *"Go, your faith has healed you."* Bartimaeus means "son of Timaeus," and Timaeus means "honor." As Bartimaeus threw off the cloak that he had wrapped himself in for so long and stepped up to Jesus, he was stepping forward to receive the honor that his name proclaimed.

Jesus is saying the same to each of us *"Go, your faith has healed you,"* and as He does, He is giving to each of us a spirit of revelation of His heart and of His nature.

Meditating on this story, you will discover more of the attributes of the Father. He is not distant but as close as your breath—omnipresent. He is all-knowing and caring—omniscient. And He is all-powerful—omnipotent. He knew us before we were conceived in our mother's womb and will know us through all eternity. He knows everything about us and is carefully orchestrating the things in our lives that will shape us into the image of His Son. Like Bartimaeus, we must throw off our garment of wounds and lies, of hopelessness and despair, and allow the Holy Spirit to heal our spiritual eyes so we can truly see who He is and who we are in Him. The Holy Spirit will bring us freedom and liberty and transform us into His image. You may have been rejected by your human father, yet:

"You have a Heavenly Father who loves you, who understands you, who thinks the best of you and who plans the best for you. He will never abandon you, never misunderstand you, never take sides against you and never reject you."[18]

Jesus Also Knew Rejection

He is despised and rejected by men, A Man of sorrows and acquainted with grief. And we hid, as it were, our faces from Him; He was despised, and we did not esteem Him. (Isaiah 53:3)

He came to His own, and His own did not receive Him. (John 1:11)

Jesus knew what it felt like to be rejected by men also; however, His heart would not be impacted by their rejection, for He knew where He came from and where He was going. His acceptance or rejection by men in no way affected His destiny, for at the beginning of His ministry as

He came up out of the waters at His baptism, He heard the words that all of us long to hear, "'This is My beloved Son in whom I am well pleased'" (Matt. 3:17).

The enemy can't do anything about our salvation, but if we agree with his lies, he can hinder us from fulfilling the destiny that our Father has planned for us. If we retain this false self that many of us have constructed intending to keep ourselves safe, it will lead to death of destiny and purpose. But if we expose the false self and allow the Lord to heal us, He will set us free from those things that have wounded and captured our hearts—free to love and trust the Father.

To Heal the Brokenhearted

Alan Chambers' Testimony

In 1972 Robert and Betty Chambers welcomed their sixth and last child into the world. I, Alan Manning Chambers, was the second huge surprise for this family having been born six years after the first surprise … who was born eight years after child number four….

When it was all said and done, my parents could say that they'd had at least one child in every decade from the '40s to the '70s. My folks … were already grandparents when I came along. They had a son in college, two kids in high school, and a kindergartener. That's some spread.

The dynamics of my life are nothing short of God ordained…. My upbringing was amazing and traumatic all at the same time. My family was anything but ordinary, and it has taken me almost my entire 41 years of life (here in 2013) to be incredibly thankful for every single bit of it.

My dad was career Air Force but retired two years before I was born. As a busy and successful chef and restaurateur, my dad traveled extensively opening new restaurants for a hotel chain. When he was home he wasn't a happy man. He was verbally abusive … to everyone. I will never forget a shopping outing where he verbally assaulted a woman in a parking lot for how she parked her car. He did end up apologizing, which taught me quite a bit, but the altercation was just one of a million similarly embarrassing moments that I endured throughout my childhood. It was compounded when that assault was on me while out in public.

A Vow

I determined very early in life that I did not want to be anything like my father. The very man that God created to be my example and role model was one I had no interest in learning anything from. Instead I latched on to my June Cleaver-like mother and distanced myself from my Archie Bunker-like dad….

Around the age of ten, an older teenage boy took advantage of me sexually. I was confused. The incident was painful in a way, but it also seemed to meet a need and answered some questions I had been asking God and myself. Am I gay? I realized that I must be—simply because I longed for another sexual encounter. I had needs that were God-given. I needed the attention, affirmation, and acceptance of a man, and I thought sex was the way to get it. It was an illegitimate way to get a legitimate need met. But to the man who is hungry, even what is bitter tastes sweet. Being molested didn't make me gay. Having a troubled relationship with my dad didn't make me gay. But the combination of the two certainly did create a deep hunger within an already emotionally starving young man.

I battled these feelings silently for the remainder of my childhood and into college. As a Christian (I gave my heart to Jesus irrevocably at the young age of six) who was entrenched in the Church I knew that I could never tell anyone of my struggles with same-sex attraction. Everyone knows the Church of the 1980s –1990s was especially derelict in showing grace, mercy, and compassion to "those people." I knew all too well what would happen and I couldn't risk my life for the sake of honesty.

One January weekend in 1991 my youth/college group went to a retreat. On the last night of the event the speaker mentioned homosexuality in a way that entreated me to go forward. I did and I confessed my feelings to that speaker. To my astonishment he did share a word of compassion and he gave me hope. He told me that God loved me and that He had a plan. That night I learned that God wasn't afraid of my struggles or me.

Ironically, around the same time, my parents came home from their church one Sunday and shared that a man from their congregation had given his testimony, which included the fact that he had lived a double life as both a gay and married man. Without divulging my own secret I asked as many questions of them as I could. They told me his name and I remember going to the pictorial directory from their church and staring at his photo and contact information wishing I had the courage to call him.

Some months later I also learned that there was a ministry serving Christians with same-sex attractions that helped provide answers, encouragement, and support as they surrendered their struggles to the Lordship of Jesus Christ. That ministry, Exodus International, had a local group in my hometown. When I called them for help I found out the man from my parents' church was the director. So God! About a year later I attended my first Exodus International Freedom Conference where nearly 1,000 people just like me showed up to worship, hear testimonies, and learn about how to live a life surrendered to Christ…. There amongst honest, desperate, humble believers … I found Christ and a beautiful example of His Bride.

On the last day of that conference I was sitting in the balcony of the chapel…. Before the service let out, however, God began speaking to my heart. My dad was the focus of the conversation … God the Father first comforted me. My dad had been a bear to live with and God the Father told me how sorry He was that I had endured such pain…. But God the Father went further saying specifically, "Your pain, however, doesn't matter more to me than your dad's pain. He has been hurt, too, and that is why he's treated you in the way that he has."…God continued. "Stop thinking of yourself as a hurt child and your dad as a mean father. Start thinking of him as your brother who has endured far more pain than you could ever bear or imagine. Forgive him."

In that moment, my heart shattered into a million tiny pieces. For some reason I knew that God the Father was both perfectly good and being honest about the pain my dad had endured. My heart broke for him, and my unforgiveness and bitterness flowed in the tears that were pouring down my face. God the Father healed a broken little boy's heart that day, and I have never been bitter again.

I went home from the conference and told my parents that I needed to talk with them. In the living room where I had grown up I started by saying, "Dad, you were a very hard man to live with, and some of the ways you treated me made it very difficult to love you. But, I have forgiven you and hope you will forgive me for holding onto bitterness and anger and hatred. I know your life hasn't been easy, and that you were doing the best you could."

At that point my dad apologized, owned his faults, and then shared what he had never shared with anyone. The pain that God the Father told me my dad had endured began to pour out of my dad's mouth…horrific stories of abuse that he had suffered and of the shame that made him the strict military man that he was. It was nothing short of a miracle that he was able to survive the abuse he endured let alone the retelling of it that day. When he was finished, we all cried.

My dad, who was completely retired by that time, cried for weeks after. He sat in a chair most days looking out our front window. He was different, quiet, broken. I asked my mom if the revelation of my same-sex attractions were what seemed to be causing this stillness or if I had hurt him that day. She said that he had never been more proud of anyone than he was of me and the courage of what I had shared. She said that his demeanor was reflective of the pain that he had caused and that he needed time to work through it and then move on. His quietness lasted over a month, and then he emerged a very different man.

There wasn't a day that went by after that summer in 1993 that my dad didn't call me to tell me how much he loved me…. He called all of my siblings daily, and he treated my mother as his most prized treasure…. I have to admit, I did not always know what to do with his sweet side. The transformation was amazing, though.

My dad was in poor health even then, but it got progressively worse. My parents' bedroom was converted into one that accommodated his hospital bed. There were days when my dad was too sick to talk much. On those days he would just look at me and hold my hand. His gaze was one of deep, deep love and pride. Where I had once felt only disappointment from him, I now felt as if I was the one he loved the most. My joys were his joys, and my sorrow was his sorrow. I knew beyond a shadow of a doubt that I was my father's son and that he loved me beyond words.

n 1998 I married my dearest Leslie and my dad was so proud. After years of struggling with infertility and the deep pain of that, Leslie and I adopted two newborns, a boy and a girl, in 2005…. His love for my children, my wife, and me was palpable.

In late April of 2007, we were called home early from a trip. My dad, having endured two decades of illness, decided to stop dialysis…. My sisters and I stayed at the house with my parents for three days. People came and went like a reunion. The house was as a house should be, full of life, love, stories, and amazing food…. Old friends visited and called, and my dad told stories that we were determined to remember. It was a special time.

On May 2, 2007, just before I went to sleep in my childhood bedroom, I quickly got up and went into my parents' dark room, touched my dad, and said, "I love you, Daddy." He looked at me and said, "I love you, son."

The next morning he didn't wake up…. By lunchtime we were all gathered around his bed—all of his kids and his one wife of 54 years. My wife and children were there, too. My mom spoke to him in his ear and said things that only a lifelong companion can say, I imagine. As she finished, my dad left us and joined God the Father. It was one of the single most beautiful and gut-wrenching moments of my life…. It will always be a precious gift.

In the six years since my father's death, I have done a lot of thinking. I have realized that I am so my father's son. I have realized that I never wanted to be a man until the day my father showed me his heart and shared his pain with me. I have realized that I want to be like my dad and love my wife and kids the way my dad did those last 14 years of his life. I have realized that God the Father is so good, so trustworthy, so tender and that my dad was an amazing example of Him.

Forgiveness changed me and showed me God the Father in a way that I could have never seen or known had I not first endured the pain and then been healed.

๛๛๛๛

Then He who sat on the throne said, "Behold, I make all things new." (Rev. 21:5)

This profound statement is made by the Author of Life. Christ, the author and finisher of our faith, is the only One who can make all things new, based on the finished work of the Cross. Because He paid the price through the labor of the Cross, He is able to offer new life to whosoever will come. It doesn't matter where we have been; what matters is that it is true. And it is His desire that we all receive of this profound truth. Like Alan, all of mankind suffers because they long for reconciliation with their Father.

Since the world began, man has repeatedly made mistakes. He has blatantly sinned without thinking about it because it is just part of his nature. From the very day they were placed outside of the garden, things did not go smoothly for Adam and Eve. They lived in the world as orphans, stumbling blindly through life like blind Bartimaeus, and so did all of their descendants. But God had a plan to rescue man.

All of the testimonies and all of the encounters shared throughout the pages of this book have a common theme—these people suffered immeasurably from the lives they were living, but when they encountered Jesus they found the way to freedom. As we've progressed on our journey, we have seen different ways that the orphan spirit has worked in peoples' lives. We have seen a few of the many attributes of God in His interactions with them to set them free.

God's plan to rescue man was put into action at the Cross. Through the Cross, God provided a way to change us back from orphans into beloved children of the Most-High God.

CHAPTER 15

THE CROSS

The Father's Love Shown in the Beauty of the Cross

When I consider the Cross, I think of Easter and the joy of an empty tomb. Jesus conquered death—the one thing that all humankind fears. The Cross was God's greatest display of love as He came in the flesh and suffered the penalty for our sins in our place. What marvelous grace the Father has lavished on each one of us! By believing in the Lord Jesus Christ, each one of us has become a beloved son or daughter of the Most-High God. It's amazing! But there are many that haven't yet found or entered into that truth.

Let God break the power of the lies of the enemy that have so bound you and held you back from entering into an intimate relationship with Him.

For by one offering He has perfected forever those who are being sanctified. (Heb. 10:14)

Jesus' body on the Cross is that "offering He has perfected forever." The offering is perfected, but He continues to sanctify us.

"The key to God's favor doesn't rest on what I give Him, but on what He has already given me."[19]

"The Lord your God in your midst, The Mighty One, will save; He will rejoice over you with gladness, He will quiet you with His love, He will rejoice over you with singing." (Zeph. 3:17)

If we view the Cross as God only satisfying His justice, then we unconsciously empty the Cross of its power. The redemptive work of the Cross will result in God making all things new.

In his book, *What's So Amazing About Grace* (2008, Zondervan), Philip Yancey wrote about a prostitute he had interviewed in Chicago. She declared, "Church! Why would I ever go there? I already feel terrible about myself. They just make me feel worse!" What a shame that she should feel that way. The very place where she should be able to go for help and safety brings condemnation instead.

"But I am convinced the dissonant perspectives about God that result from an appeasement based view of the cross, cause many to shy away from the intimate relationship He seeks with us."
"Since Adam's fall we have come to picture God not as a loving Father inviting us to trust Him, but an exacting sovereign who must be appeased. When we start from that vantage point we miss God's purpose on the cross. For His plan was not to satisfy some need in Himself at His Son's expense, but rather to satisfy a need in us at His own expense."[20]

Instead of seeing God as a loving Father, people fear Him as an angry judge. They think they have to fix themselves before they can come to church and get to know God, not realizing that they need God's help in order to change what's wrong in them.

For what the law could not do in that it was weak through the flesh, God did by sending His own Son in the likeness of sinful flesh, on account of sin: He condemned sin in the flesh. (Rom. 8:3)

I had totally misunderstood the Christian faith. I came to see that it was in my brokenness and powerlessness and my weakness that Jesus was made strong. It was in the acceptance of my lack of faith that God could give me faith.[21]

As I consider the Cross, I begin to see the Father's heart. I hear Him say, "Come follow Me." This is the way to freedom; this is the way to life that springs forth from the most horrible death ever experienced by a man—the death of the Son of God.

What God desires is our hearts; hearts responding to His unconditional love for us. When we give Him our hearts in absolute abandon and trust, then we will walk in obedience as a child of God. It is a simple transaction, but it seems difficult to our very human nature. Our flesh wars against the Spirit, yet our spirits yearn to follow our Father's leading. For we know that when we do, we will walk in absolute freedom and liberty as the sons and daughters of God.

The redemptive plan of God was fully implemented by the finished work of the Cross that Jesus completed for all mankind. The victory of the Cross was over all principalities, powers, and over death, to fully satisfy the justice of God through the death of His Son and to make a way for us to be reconciled to God. This great plan of redemption was initiated before the foundation of the world.

The Cross is the greatest expression of God's unconditional love for us. It is a revelation of the servant heart of God. The redemptive plan of God was implemented at the Cross and will be fully realized in the age to come. In Revelation 21:5, Jesus declares, *"Behold I make all things new."* God fully restores and redeems all things. The justice of God at the Cross made provision for those things bent and twisted by sin in order that all would be restored to their original design. When we respond to the Gospel of the Lord Jesus Christ, we become sons and daughters of God.

"The cross of Christ is the revealed truth of God's judgment on sin. It was the supreme triumph and it shook the very foundation of hell." By the Cross we have joined with Christ in co-resurrection and co-eternal life. "The eternal life that was in Jesus becomes ours because of the Cross once we make the decision to be identified with Him."[22]

When we look at the Cross and see the great suffering, we must understand that all three members of the Trinity—Father, Son, and Holy Spirit—were fully involved and entered together into the cost of the Cross. Then we can begin to observe God's compassion and mercy for all humanity. We see the heart of God desiring to meet the needs of fallen mankind and realize that He and He alone could do that as the pure and spotless Lamb of God.

As we look back to the Garden of Eden, we hear the voice of God declaring to Satan, *"He shall bruise your head."* But there, in the midst of great disappointment and an atmosphere of hopelessness, the mercy and compassion of God for those He created in His image is fully expressed. As our gaze moves forward in time to the Cross, we realize the full meaning of those words. Those standing by and observing thought it was great weakness and apparent failure when Jesus gave His life on the cross. But in willingly laying down His life, He fully satisfied the justice of God, displaying the unconditional love of God to all mankind, and utterly defeating Satan.

The Apostle Paul wrote:

He who did not spare His own Son, but delivered Him up for us all, how shall He not with Him also freely give us all things? (Rom. 8:32)

When we gaze upon the Cross, we observe the suffering heart of God expressing fully the compassionate mercy of God—*that* is the Father's heart.

It is imperative that we are not just casual observers of this Man hanging from the tree. We must allow the Holy Spirit to unveil our eyes in order that our hearts can be captured by such infinite, eternal love for us. The world can never imitate or produce this love; it only comes from the great heart of our Eternal Father.

We see God using this greatest of sacrifices to prepare a bride for His Son. Just as Adam lay sleeping while God removed a rib from his side in order to create Eve, his bride, so out of the wounded side of Jesus would come forth His pure and spotless bride. It is a bride washed in the eternal blood of Christ; a bride who would walk before her Beloved with no compromise and in absolute confidence in her Lord.

At the cross, the Father provided for Himself an eternal family. He adopted those who would believe in His Only Begotten Son as His heirs—joint-heirs with His Eternal Son.

Chosen in Him before the foundation of the world, we who have by faith believed in the only begotten Son of God and in His redemptive labor on the cross are those sons and daughters of the Father—fully loved, even in our weakness. In the midst of great suffering, the Father heart of God was fully demonstrated. As we stand looking up at this beautiful Man, suffering and dying, we begin to see the heart of a humble God, not a God who is far off or distant, but one who in every way has suffered in order that

He might be our great High Priest, One who is able to help us in our greatest trials.

> *For we do not have a High Priest who cannot sympathize with our weaknesses, but was in all points tempted as we are, yet without sin. (Hebrews 4:15)*

In the midst of excruciating pain, the heart of God is demonstrated as He provides for us the way to be reconciled to our Heavenly Father. We must allow the Holy Spirit to reveal to our hearts the tremendous cost of the Cross and the absolute willingness of God to humble Himself in order to redeem us.

Observing the Cross, we see the holiness and purity of God. Once again we see our Savior in such unimaginable pain and suffering; yet, all the while we see His concern which issues forth from his pure heart for others. Not only do we see Jesus making provision for His mother, but we also see Him praying for God to have mercy and forgive those who have inflicted this pain and suffering on Him. He never utters a word of anger but only words of life, springing forth from an absolutely pure and holy heart. If we take time to observe, our hearts will be gripped by the great love of the Father even in the midst of His great suffering.

Freedom in Christ

Jesus paid the price for our sins when He died on the cross. When we come to Him in repentance, the blood that He shed washes away our sin—never to be remembered anymore. With it comes glorious freedom! No longer do we need to labor under a heavy burden of guilt. We do not have to be afraid of what God will think of us. He sees us as righteous and not guilty—this is the provision He has made for us.

His Cross is the door by which every member of the human race can enter into the life of God; by His resurrection, He has the right to give eternal life to anyone, and by His ascension, our Lord entered heaven keeping the door open for humanity.[23]

Stand fast therefore in the liberty by which Christ has made us free, and do not be entangled again with a yoke of bondage. (Gal. 5:1)

He has given us the opportunity to be forever free. Like the Galatians, we have been set free to rest in who we are in Him and to become all that God has destined us to be—to rest secure in His finished work. He has set us free to rest in His eternal favor; free to love and be loved.

Paul wrote this verse in Galatians 5 because he had heard that the believers in Galatia, after having been saved by grace through faith, were returning to the works of the Law. They had been deceived by some who had entered into their midst and convinced them that they must observe the works of the Law in order to maintain their salvation. As a result, some of these believers were getting circumcised. The enemy had convinced them that they would have to perform works in order to maintain their salvation. They didn't realize who they were or who their Heavenly Father was. Nor did they recognize the amazing work that Christ had accomplished on the cross for them—a work that was *completely finished*.

They were reacting like orphans instead of beloved sons and daughters of God. Their hearts had been captured—they had forgotten that when they came into the kingdom they were no longer captive, but had been set free.

The Truth Will Set You Free

The revelation of the Father's heart was given to us in order to set us free.

The encounters Jesus had with individuals, parables He spoke, and every story He shared were for the purpose of setting those created in His image free. To believe otherwise is to believe a lie. When we agree with a lie, we empower it to have its way in our lives, ensnaring and entrapping us and inhibiting our destiny in God. However, believing and acting on God's Word sets us free! Jesus said,

> *"And you shall know the truth and the truth shall make you free." (John 8:32)*

When we walk in the freedom that was purchased for us at the Cross and in relationship with our Heavenly Father, we will discover who we really are. Freedom brings with it the power to become all that God created us to be. As joint heirs with Christ, all that God has is ours. This freedom liberates us to walk as Jesus walked in a continual intimate relationship with the Father, being fully aware of what He is doing and saying. If we could fully grasp the freedom that was paid for at the cross, we would soar in all that God has destined us to be.

Freedom Empowers Us

As we abide in this freedom found in Christ, we will discover the purpose and destiny for which we were created. From the very beginning of time, God desired for His sons and daughters to fill the earth, subdue it, and have dominion over His creation, bringing heaven to earth.

God allowed Satan to be on the earth when He created man. It was God's plan for man to take dominion over the earth, releasing heaven and the kingdom of God on earth, thereby destroying the works of the evil one. That place of great authority was stolen in the garden through deception, but Christ won it back. The night that Jesus was betrayed, He said these words to His disciples, and they are for us as well:

> *"…he who believes in Me, the works that I do he will do also; and greater works than these he will do, because I go to My Father." (John 14:12)*

The Hope of God

When we meditate upon the Cross and what the Lord Jesus accomplished there, our hearts are gripped with hope, a hope that the world can never give or imagine. It is a confidence in the work of redemption. The labor of Christ causes our hearts to be filled with joy, knowing that God made a way for all mankind to be reconciled to the Father. It brings hope that promises that He *"…will make all things new,"* and that we can be totally secure in that truth. The Apostle Paul wrote:

> *Now may the God of hope fill you with all joy and peace in believing, that you may abound in hope by the power of the Holy Spirit. (Romans 15:13)*

When we come to Christ as believers, by faith, our sin is paid for and the power of sin is broken. He didn't do this for just one person; He did it for the whole world.

> *And He Himself is the propitiation for our sins, and not for ours only but also for the whole world. (1 John 2:2)*

The word propitiation carries the basic idea of appeasement, or satisfaction, specifically towards God. Propitiation is a two-part act that involves appeasing the wrath of an offended person and being reconciled to him. When we believe in the Lord Jesus and become His followers, *we no longer have to be afraid of God's wrath.*

Redemption is not only payment made for our sins, to take away our sins, but as our Redeemer, Jesus Christ is our protector and defender.

> And you know that He was manifested to take away our sins, and in Him there is no sin. (1 John 3:5)

Jesus is our advocate. *He stands before the Father declaring our innocence through His blood.*

> My little children, these things I write to you, so that you may not sin. And if anyone sins, we have an Advocate with the Father, Jesus Christ the righteous. (1 John 2:1)

Hebrews repeatedly refers to Jesus as our great High Priest. Jesus is the One who said, "'I will never leave you nor forsake you.'" Not leaving us orphaned, but watching out for us, He promised to send the Holy Spirit, the promise of the Father.

Scars are the result of wounds, caused by an accident or physical abuse or maybe the result of the misuse use of words. Each of us has scars—both inward and outward ones. They can become something of beauty or they can become something of great deformity. Reading Isaiah 53, we are confronted with the reality of the unconditional love of God. Isaiah 53 is a Messianic prophecy pointing to Christ. We have a picture of Christ portraying the wounds or scars of the cross hundreds of years before He would actually be nailed there. If we allow the Holy Spirit to bring revelation to us concerning His scars, we will fall before this beautiful Man, Christ Jesus, in absolute gratitude for what He did for each of us in order that we might come into an intimate relationship with our Heavenly Father.

The longer you gaze at His scars, the more beautiful He becomes. Appreciation for His love and beauty overwhelms you, and you are drawn to the scars, not repulsed by them—for they represent his unconditional covenant love for each one of us.

In the Apostle Paul's writings, he says that for me to know Him I must come into fellowship with His sufferings, and only God can orchestrate this. The greatest suffering I have faced to this point in my life is the loss of Pam. It created in me the greatest wound I've ever experienced; however, the way I choose to respond to this wounding may result in one of two things. I will either enter into the power of His Resurrection—the fruit of Christ being the evidence of that—or into the power of the world, that leads to bitterness, anger, resentment, judgment, and death. I choose the former. Painful though it may be, I desire people to see the scars from this wound in my life and, when they see it, to smell the sweet fragrance of Christ.

I want my life to make a difference—not just for one generation—but for multiple generations. I want to reflect the Father's heart, impacting the lives of those around me—not by *my* words but by His words and mighty deeds *through* me. If you want that, too, then fully embracing the Cross is the way to the Father's heart.

Recently I met with someone who was in a major accident years ago and was left with a quite evident scar. But as I heard the individual's story and looked at the scar, it by no means detracted from the person's beauty—it only enhanced it. When we embrace Jesus, suffering can make us into God's image—and that is just what happened with this person.

When I hear the stories of Jesus and gaze at His scars, His love overwhelms me. Each of us has a story to tell. None of us can escape this life without scars as a result of wounds, but when we are wounded, we must turn to the One who was wounded for us, lean into His arms, and allow Him to bring not only healing, but "beauty for ashes." As wounds and scars bring change, allow them to make you "a life changer" for the kingdom of God.

God Provided a Way of Reconciliation

> *Blessed be the God and Father of our Lord Jesus Christ, who has blessed us with every spiritual blessing in the heavenly places in Christ, just as He chose us in Him before the foundation of the world, that we should be holy and without blame before Him in love, having predestined us to adoption as sons by Jesus Christ to Himself, according to the good pleasure of His will, to the praise of the glory of His grace, by which He made us accepted in the Beloved. In Him we have redemption through His blood, the forgiveness of sins, according to the riches of His grace which He made to abound toward us in all wisdom and prudence, having made known to us the mystery of His will, according to His good pleasure which He purposed in Himself, that in the dispensation of the fullness of the times He might gather together in one all things in Christ, both which are in heaven and which are on earth—in Him. (Eph. 1:3-10)*

God's heart has always been (and still is) to provide a way for all of mankind to be reconciled with Him. Back in the garden at the beginning of time, God had already devised a plan to rescue man from his wayward thoughts and deeds; it was through the Cross and the Cross *alone* that God made a way for us all. We must remember that the Cross not only provided a way for our sins to be forgiven but also for our lives to be redeemed and restored in every way. The enemy would have you believe that you must do something in order to appease God, yet God became flesh, and through His Son, did what no one else could do, bearing the sins of all mankind and the retribution of God in our place.

The primary goal of Jesus' earthly ministry was to

bring us into the same loving relationship with the Father that exists between the Father and Son. The Father sent His Son to reconcile us with Himself and to help us experience the same great love that He has for His Son. Just hours before going to the Cross, Jesus prayed about this for you and me.

> *"O righteous Father! The world has not known You, but I have known You; and these have known that You sent Me. And I have declared to them Your name, and will declare it, that the love with which You loved Me may be in them, and I in them." (John 17:2-26)*

In this prayer, we understand that Jesus is continuing to reveal God as our Father in order for us to know that we are loved by the Father with the same love that He has for His Son. As we walk in this revelation, the same love that Jesus has for the Father will be reciprocated with others. Our fear of being rejected is overcome by a revelation of the unconditional love of the Father for each of us.

Isaiah 42:1-3 has been foundational in this book. God told us in this passage that He had put His Spirit upon His Elect One, His Servant. Jesus expressed the fullness of the Father and in so doing represented His Spirit which reflected the Father's nature and character. It says also that Jesus will bring justice. That is what the Cross provides and that is what He does in our lives as we surrender to Him those things that have so negatively impacted our lives.

In his book, *He Loves Me: Learning to Live in the Father's Affections,* Wayne Jacobsen tells the story about a hen and her chicks that were caught in a forest fire. Seeing there was no escape for her or her little chicks, the mother covered her babies with her body, only to be killed by the fire. Later after the fire burned out, firefighters discovered her.

As they removed her body, they discovered that the little chicks had survived the fire, protected by their mother.

As he finishes this story, Jacobsen goes on to say: "The Creator of heaven and earth did exactly the same thing, by the Cross, in order to rescue His wayward children from their own destruction" (*He Loves Me: Learning to Live in the Father's Affections, 2008, Windblown Media*).

> *Greater love has no one than this, than to lay down one's life for his friends. (John 15:13)*

In laying down His life that we might live, God demonstrated the ultimate sacrificial love, providing redemption and reconciliation and restoring us as sons and daughters of our Heavenly Father. *We are no longer orphans; we are His beloved children!*

END NOTES

1. Quote from the movie *Patch Adams,* 1998, Universal Studios

2. Victor Hugo, *Les Miserables*, 1862

3. Clark Whitten, *Pure Grace: The Life Changing Power of Uncontaminated Grace*, 2012, Destiny Image Publishers, Inc.

4. A. W. Tozer, *The Pursuit of God,* 1997, Christian Publications

5. Wayne Jacobsen, *He Loves Me: Learning to Live in the Father's Affections,* 2008, Windblown Media

6. Oswald Chambers, *My Utmost for His Highest, The Nature of Regeneration,* 2014, Discovery House Publishers

7. Oswald Chambers, *My Utmost for His Highest: The Forgiveness of God*, 2014

8. Wayne Jacobson, *He Loves Me: Learning to Live in the Father's Affections*, 2008, Windblown Media

9. Bill Johnson, Senior Pastor, Bethel Church, Redding, California

10. Used with permission from an interview given by Paul Young

11. Wayne Jacobsen, *He Loves Me: Learning to Live in the Father's Affections,* 2008, Windblown Media

12. Rudolf Bultmann, "Mercy" *Theological Dictionary of the New Testament*, 1964, Grand Rapids, Mich.: Eerdmans, 2:477-87

13. Wayne Jacobson, *He Loves Me: Learning to Live in the Father's Affections,* 2008, Windblown Media

14. Oswald Chambers, *My Utmost for His Highest*, 2014, Discovery House Publishers

15. Andy and Janine Mason, *Dream Culture*

16. A. W. Pink, *The Attributes of God,* Chapter 16, The Love of God

17. Brennan Manning, *Lion and Lamb*, 1986, Chosen Books, pg. 64

18. Derek Prince, *God's Remedy for Rejection*, 2002, Whitaker House

19. Wayne Jacobson, *He Loves Me: Learning to Live in the Father's Affections*, 2008, Windblown Media

20. Wayne Jacobson, *He Loves Me: Learning to Live in the Father's Affections*, 2008, Windblown Media, Page 104

21. Brennan Manning, *Abba's Child*, 2014, NavPress

22. Oswald Chambers, *My Utmost for His Highest*, 2014, Discovery House Publishers

23. Oswald Chambers, *My Utmost for His Highest*, 2014, Discovery House Publishers